Praise for Terry Eagleton

The Event of Literature

"Shrewd, authoritative, and very readable—this is Eagleton at his best." —Jonathan Culler

Reason, Faith, and Revolution: Reflections on the God Debate

"Jaunty and surprisingly entertaining." —John Banville, *Irish Times*

The Truth About the Irish

"A fine, fast and very funny meditation." —*Washington Post*

The Idea of Culture

"A Voice of sanity amid the roar of turbo–capitalism." —*Independent*

ACROSS the POND

An Englishman's View of America

Terry Eagleton

W. W. NORTON & COMPANY

NEW YORK   LONDON

For information about permission to reproduce selections from this book,
write to Permissions, W. W. Norton & Company, Inc.,
500 Fifth Avenue, New York, NY 10110

For information about special discounts for bulk purchases, please contact
W. W. Norton Special Sales at specialsales@wwnorton.com or 800-233-4830

Manufacturing by Courier Westford
Book design by Ellen Cipriano
Production manager: Louise Mattarelliano

Library of Congress Cataloging-in-Publication Data

Eagleton, Terry, 1943–
  Across the pond : an Englishman's view of America / Terry Eagleton. — First
edition.
     pages cm
  ISBN 978-0-393-08898-4 (hardcover)
  1. Popular culture—United States. 2. British—United States—Anecdotes.
3. Eagleton, Terry, 1943-—Travel—United States. 4. Popular culture—
Great Britain. 5. United States—Social life and customs. 6. Great Britain—
Social life and customs. 7. National characteristics, American. 8. National
characteristics, British. 9. English language—Variation—United States.
10. English language—Variation—Great Britain. I. Title.
  E169.Z83E24 2013
  306.0973—dc23
                    2013000340

ISBN 978-0-393-34940-5 pbk.

W. W. Norton & Company, Inc.
500 Fifth Avenue, New York, N.Y. 10110
www.wwnorton.com

W. W. Norton & Company Ltd.
Castle House, 75/76 Wells Street, London W1T 3QT

1 2 3 4 5 6 7 8 9 0

For

Maud Ellmann

and

Annie Janowitz

Contents

ACROSS the POND

Introduction

Since I shall have some critical things to say about Americans in this book, as well as some admiring ones, I had better begin by pointing out that some of my best friends are Americans. My wife and three of my children, for example. It is true that they are hardly typical Americans, belonging as they do to that minority of U.S. citizens who have not been abducted by aliens. It is remarkable what bias aliens display in choosing their abductees. For some unfathomable reason, Americans get to be whisked off to other galaxies far more often than, say, Swedes or Slovenes. Perhaps the United Nations might be persuaded to pass a motion deploring this blatant favouritism. It might insist that aliens abduct a more representative sample of the human race, paying due attention to gender, ethnicity and sexual predilection, as well as striking a balance between the developed and less developed parts of the world. Otherwise creatures from outer space are in danger of gaining themselves a reputation as Western supremacists. A more discerning approach of this kind would surely bring the extraterrestrials some scientific benefits.

They would, for example, be less likely to conclude that all human beings chew constantly on some kind of sticky substance, or shriek "Oh my God!" every time the visitors venture out of their spacecraft.

I have drawn a good deal in this book on Alexis de Tocqueville's great study, *Democracy in America*. Its insights into the country can still prove startlingly accurate. Some of its observations, it is true, might strike us today as a little awry. De Tocqueville maintains, for example, that Americans respect the marriage bond more than any other people, and place great trust in their lawyers. Even so, one has to admire the prognostic powers of a man who can write in 1835 that America and Russia "seem called by some secret design of Providence one day to hold in [their] hands the destinies of half the world." Nostradamus never managed anything half as impressive. There are other points where de Toqueville gets things right but the wrong way round. One day, he predicts, North America will be called on "to provide for the wants of the South Americans," which is not quite the case. It is South Americans who have provided for the wants of North Americans, though de Tocqueville could not be expected to be clairvoyant about neo-colonialism and crack cocaine.

"A foreigner," writes this supreme observer of American mores, "will gladly agree to praise much in their country, but he would like to be allowed to criticise something, and that he is absolutely refused." He finds this "irritable patriotism" the most irritating feature of everyday American life. Charles Dickens thought much the same. It is true that one can still find traces of this touchiness today. Several U.S. publishers were reluctant to take on this book for what one suspects were exactly such reasons. They seem not to have noticed that it is quite as hard on the British as it is on Americans. Some U.S. citizens greet even the mildest European criticism of their country with a raucous reminder that they won the Second World War for us. This is not exactly true, but not all Americans have a knowledge of history to rival a Princeton professor's. The fact that so many of them say "the eighteen hundreds" rather than "the nineteenth century" suggests that they also have an uncertain grasp of a rather basic arithmetical operation. In general, however, Americans these days are more open to being told of the odd imperfection in their culture than in de Tocqueville's time. In fact, there are some in the country who are almost pathologically prepared to believe the very worst about themselves. This is to do themselves quite as much an injustice as to boast that they are God's gift to humanity. But Americans find it hard to do things by halves.

On the Usefulness of Stereotypes

Can one, however, speak of Americans in this grandly generalising way? Is this not the sin of stereotyping, which all high-minded liberals have learnt to abhor? There are, after all, a good many Americans, of various shapes and sizes, and it is hard to see how these millions of unique individuals can be reduced to a single type. Stereotyping is a particularly contentious issue in the United States, largely because of the country's ethnic divisions. But it is also frowned on because America is probably the most individualist nation on earth, with a firm conviction that every one of its citizens is special. Nobody falls into a general category. Everyone is his or her own elite. As a character in a Henry James novel proudly puts it, "We are all princes here." The whole nation is a winner. Or at least, those who are not actually winners are en route to becoming so, as an egg is en route to becoming a chicken.

Quite how everyone can be special without nobody being so is a problem we can leave to the logicians. Can everybody really be special, any more than everybody can win the New York Marathon? In a society where everyone is special, being special would seem to be nothing special. It is true that people are unique, in the sense that they are themselves and not somebody else. This, however, is not necessarily a virtue. The Boston Strangler, for instance, would probably have been a great deal better off being someone else. Some Americans might even feel the same about one or two of their recent presidents.

If Americans jealously safeguard their individuality, then this, ironically, is a general fact about them. It is a truth which applies to all these supposedly incomparable individuals, which means that they cannot really be incomparable after all. Besides, if we were not able to stereotype each other with a fair degree of accuracy, social life would grind to a halt. We would not be able to cope with the myriad different situations we encounter if we did not subsume them under certain general categories. There are certain predictable social patterns, such as the iron law which states that in any British café which places salt, pepper, a milk jug and a sugar bowl on each table, there will always be one table where one of these items is missing, and that this table will be your own. Sociologists are not really interested in individuals, any more than Stalinists are, which is one reason why conservatives tend to disapprove of them. They betray the shameful secret that almost everything we do has been done millions of times before, and may well be done millions of times again. The words "I love you" are always at some level a quotation. All language is generalising, including words like "this," "here," "unique," "right now," and "my utterly special little sweetheart." The word "individual" originally meant "indivisible," meaning that to be a person was to be part of a greater whole. There could never be simply one person, any more than there could simply be one letter or one number.

We can deduce an alarming amount about individuals from the sparsest bits of information about them. To know that someone is female is to know that it is possible but unlikely that she will end up running the Pentagon. A child born into the Murdoch dynasty is unlikely to become a Trotskyist. Someone called O'Donovan could probably give a better account of papal infallibility than someone named Rosenheim. People with very small feet tend to know less about ancient history than people with larger feet, since toddlers are less knowledgeable about the topic than adults. Men are far more likely to throw people through windows than women. Black working-class Britons have a far greater chance of becoming mentally ill than Keira Knightley. A regular reader of the British *Guardian* newspaper is unlikely to believe that the solution to gang warfare in the North of England is to detonate a small nuclear weapon over Bradford. People in Butte, Montana, are not typically dandies and aesthetes who lounge languidly around town wearing loose crimson garments and reciting aloud from Dante's *Purgatorio*, or at least those who do would be well advised to walk warily at night. Wearing fishnet stockings and calling yourself Saucy Sally is not the kind of thing to get you elected governor of South Carolina, not least if you happen to be a man.

Stereotypes are often thought to be negative and demeaning. But this is not always true. Some of them are, while others are anything but. The Irish do not take kindly to being told that they are dirty, idle, feckless, lying, drunken, priest-ridden brawlers, apart from the odd masochist among them who might find this censure a touch too mild. For some mysterious reason, this kind of language tends to make them rather cross. Yet many Irish people are rather gratified to be told that they are genial, charming, witty, eloquent, poetic and hospitable, even though this is just as much of a stereotype. This may not make stereotyping any more acceptable in some people's eyes, but it complicates the issue. In any case, stereotypes need not deny that we are all distinctive individuals. It is just that, like medical textbooks or prayers for the dying, they focus on what we have in common. To attend only to differences would be as misleading as to see nothing but similarities.

Let us take a case in point. An American friend of mine once confessed to me that he found a certain philosopher rather standoffish. I told him that he had the word almost correct: it wasn't standoffish, it was Scottish. Scottish men tend to smile less than American men do, a fact that can easily be mistaken for churlishness. In fact, a male Scot will probably smile only faintly if he meets you after a twenty-year absence and you are his mother. On the whole, Scots are less emotionally expressive than Americans, which is not of course to say that they are any less emotional. There is probably more grinning per square yard in Arizona than there is in Aberdeen. Christianity for some U.S. Evangelicals seems to be mainly about grinning. The Gospel is not about being crucified but about being cheerful. Perhaps these people have stumbled on a lost version of the text, with verses such as "A new commandment I give you, that you grin at one another," or "Grin and it shall be given unto you." In Presbyterian Scotland, religion is certainly no laughing matter. Scottish unsmilingness has no doubt much to do with John Calvin and John Knox. There is nothing chromosomal about it.

People from Northern Ireland, many of whom are of Scottish descent, are generally less emotionally forthcoming than those from the Irish Republic. They do not typically engage in bouts of surreal wit or zany, slapstick comedy, which is not to say that they are in the least without humour. When it comes to cultural differences between the British and the Americans, it is notable that the British do not generally use your first name on first meeting, though the American habit of doing so is rapidly gaining ground among them. This is partly a matter of reserve, but partly also a fear of being intrusive. When I was an Oxford academic, some of my senior colleagues still addressed me by my second name after twenty years of acquaintanceship. When I was an undergraduate at Cambridge, my tutor called me Eagleton in my first year, Terence in my second, and Terry in my third. Who knows what teasingly erotic nickname he might have come up with had I stayed an extra year?

Consider these stereotyping statements:

The Irish are funny and friendly.

The British are funny but not friendly.

The Americans are friendly but not funny.

The French are neither funny nor friendly.

What is so offensive about this? The suggestion that there are no funny Americans, friendly French or unfunny Irish? But to call these statements stereotyping is to say that no such suggestion is intended. To think so would be to misunderstand the meaning of a stereotype. To claim that Chicago is a busy city is not to suggest that every square inch of the place is crammed with frenetic activity round the clock, and nobody imagines that it does. "The west of Ireland is wet" does not mean that it rains there all the time, though in fact it rains on average two days out of three. If people have shared roughly the same social and material conditions for long periods of time, it would be astonishing if they did not display certain cultural and psychological features in common. To deny this would be to suggest that their social conditions played no part in their formation, which is by and large a conservative rather than a progressive case. This is all that the phrase "national characteristics" means. It does not imply that Germans are genetically efficient, or that Italians are biologically disposed to making declarations of undying love to women they pass in the street. There is no trace of an ability to brew magnificent beer woven into in the DNA of the Belgians. And there is no doubt that a good many stereotypes are thoroughly offensive.

The same dismissal of social conditions underlies the American Dream. As long as you have enough will-power and ambition, the fact that you are a destitute Latino with a gargantuan drink problem puts you at no disadvantage to graduates of the Harvard Business School when it comes to scaling the social ladder. All you need do is try. It is to the credit of the British that they have rarely fallen for this illusion, a fact illustrated by their saying "If at first you don't succeed, try, try and then for

God's sake give up, there's no point in making a bloody fool of yourself."

One reason why so many people end up on death row in the United States is because social conditions are thought to be irrelevant to their behaviour. To plead that the killer was beaten every day of his childhood by a sadistic drug addict of a father is a shameless cop-out. Surely others suffered the same fate yet turned out to be model citizens? This is rather like claiming that because cigarettes do not kill all smokers, they play no part in killing any of them. Some Americans fear that to give social influences their due is to cave in to some kind of social determinism. But this anxiety is quite unreal. To be shaped by social factors is not to be a puppet of them. Freedom does not mean freedom from being conditioned by one's circumstances. It is only through our circumstances that we pick up the concept of freedom in the first place, as well as how to go about exercising it. A solitary individual would by no means be free. So stereotypes are in need of more defence than they customarily receive. Even so, the discerning reader will note that when I make large generalisations about the British, Irish and Americans in this book, my comments must occasionally be seen as involving a degree of poetic license and a pinch of salt.

Divided Languages

Miscommunications

I was flying on an American passenger jet from Dublin to New York at a height of thirty-five thousand feet when the flight attendant came on the intercom and announced: "Ladies and gentlemen, we're now switching off the engines, as they don't seem to be working properly." Seizing my fountain pen, I started to scribble an urgent note to a well-known English movie star, to be found later on my body. I was sorry, I wrote, that she had failed to recognise that we were soul mates. It was with regret that I noted that she had chosen a handsome, talented young millionaire movie director as a partner, rather than a more obviously suitable person like myself. Convinced that there should be complete frankness between us, I confessed that my affection for her had been sorely tried by her disgracefully self-indulgent exhibition of tears at an Oscar ceremony. I was, however, prepared to forgive her for this unseemliness, and even managed through gritted teeth to send my best wishes and farewells to her husband. It seemed imprudent to appear before the Judgement seat with hatred in my heart.

I ended by signing my name with a flourish for the last time, put on my jacket with the obscure sense that one should die with a certain formality rather than in shirtsleeves, and awaited a sickening thud. I briefly considered ordering a double whisky, but decided that it was in the best British tradition to go down with a clear head. I would raise my chin high, but not in order to pour liquor down my throat. It then occurred to me to add a postscript to my note, assuring the recipient of my unwavering devotion in the few seconds of life still granted to me, and pointing out on a more practical note that if the public ever got fed up with her and she found it hard to obtain work, I had a little money stashed away in the top drawer of my desk that she was welcome to have. If she did make use of it, a modest statue in my memory would not, I intimated, come amiss.

It was only then that I realised that my fellow passengers seemed to be greeting the flight attendant's apocalyptic announcement with remarkable *sang froid*. They were still sipping their coffees, fiddling with their headsets, and allowing their children to sport sick bags on their noses, for all the world as though they were not about to perish. When the attendant repeated his announcement, I realised that he had said they were turning off the entertainment, not the engines. His American accent had deceived me. For some of the more media-dependent passengers on the plane, this news was no doubt almost as devastating as being told that they had only four minutes to live. But at least we were going to make JFK Airport in one piece, with or without the accompaniment of Johnny Depp.

The same misunderstandings can happen the other way round. An American friend of mine was driving rather too vigorously in the west of Ireland, and was pulled over by a Gard (police officer). "What would happen if you were to run into Mr. Fog?" the Gard inquired gruffly in his thick Connaught accent. Stung by this patronising query, my friend replied with heavy sarcasm, "Well, I guess I'd put Mr. Foot on Mr. Brake." Whereupon the officer stared at him rather strangely and growled, "I said *mist or fog*." My friend, as it happens, is an anthropologist. For one enthralling moment he thought he had stumbled upon a tribe in the west of Ireland which personified aspects of the weather, speaking of Mrs. Hailstorm, Master Sunshine, and so on. Other misunderstandings are possible, too. Some years ago, an American student I taught was surprised to see British road signs reading "Way Out." I told him that they were left over from the 1960s, when there were also road signs reading "Cool," "Groovy," "Peace and Love," and the like.

I once rang an American colleague and reached his voice mail, which announced: "Hi, this is Mike and Marie. We do not reply to silly questions." Perhaps they had been besieged by callers asking them how many triangular pink objects they had in the house, or how much it cost to rent a lawn mower in Kuala Lumpur. Later I realised he had said "survey questions." Americans who are asked by immigration officers to state the purpose of their visit on arriving in the United Kingdom should be advised that some American pronunciations of "tourism" can sound quite like "terrorism." In fact, the public speeches of George W. Bush seemed to many of the British to be constantly warning against the evils of tourism. Since Bush was scarcely the most cosmopolitan president to grace the White House, this might have reflected his true opinion. Perhaps he was running the words "tourism" and "terrorism" together for reasons of economy. There can also be problems when travelling from Europe to America, since prospective visitors to the United States are now required to complete a form declaring whether they have ever been involved in committing genocide. It would be interesting to note the official response to "Can't remember" or "Not for quite a while."

The British and the Americans, George Bernard Shaw famously observed, are divided by the same language. As one who belonged to neither nation, he could be dispassionate about the matter. In fact, the differences can be exaggerated. It is true, as the old song has it, that Americans say "tomato" and the British say "tomahto," but nobody in Britain says "potahto." However, many Americans incorrectly pronounce the name "Edinburgh" to rhyme with "Marlboro." This is particularly confusing, since the British pronounce the word "Marlborough" in a way that rhymes with the correct pronunciation of "Edinburgh." British and American types of English sound alike but are also different, which is true of the two cultures as a whole. Their ways are both strange and similar to each other, a condition that Freud knew as the uncanny. It is uncanny to see something which looks familiar in outlandish guise, or to see what is foreign as though it were routine.

Every now and then, an American will reveal by a casual word or gesture that he or she is more alien than you imagined. This is rather like those science fiction movies in which the extraterrestrials appear in convincing human guise, but betray by some well-nigh imperceptible blunder—a word slightly mispronounced, a coffee cup held at a bizarre angle, a tiny drop of green blood—that they are not what they seem. At this point, a sinisterly dissonant chord will be heard on the soundtrack. In the same way, Americans can appear convincingly human to the British, only to reveal in a casual aside that they do not know how to boil an egg, brew a pot of tea, or understand the meaning of the word "fortnight." Their true otherness then flashes out in all its mind-numbing horror.

Everyone knows that when a British schoolteacher asks his boys to get out their rubbers, he is inviting them to have their erasers ready to hand, not about to give them a lesson in contraception. British people who live in flats do not set up home in burst tires. The word "bum" in Britain means buttocks, not vagrant. Americans might be interested to hear that when a British friend tells them he is going to bum a fag, he means that he is about to cadge a cigarette. An Englishman who gets through twenty fags a day is not necessarily a promiscuous homosexual. To say "I'll call you Wednesday" in British English does not mean that I shall telephone you on Wednesday, but that I shall refer to you by the name Wednesday, even if your actual name happens to be Roger or Roberta. In British English, braces keep your trousers up as well as keeping your teeth straight.

Keywords

Not all Americans know that the following words and phrases are fairly distinctive to their own brand of English: weird, awesome, reach out to, feel comfortable with, have a hard time, big time, way too much, miracle, dream, buy into, gross, closure, impact (as a transitive verb), heal, like, flunk, scary, facility, structure, blown away, I appreciate it, zero in, kind of, issue (for problem), focused, respected, determine, freaking, roil, America, momentarily, at this time, barf, kids, meet with, share with, number one, craft (as a verb), family, hacked off, bottom line, out there, bunch, totally, hero, excited, garner, aggressive (used positively), off of, empower.

Some of these terms ("weird," for example) have migrated to some extent into British English, as American speech tends to do. Another obvious example is the word "like," repeated every four seconds or so by young Americans, and now increasingly by other English speakers as well. It is rumoured that you can now find tombstones in the States reading: "To Our Beloved Son, Brother and Like Husband." There are also proposals to modernise certain time-worn slogans to "In Like God We Trust" and "My Country Like 'Tis of Thee." There will no doubt soon be headlines in *The Washington Post* reading: "I Was Like 'Oh My God!' Says President of Harvard." The pathologically compulsive use of the word "like" has much to do with a postmodern aversion to dogmatism. "It's nine o'clock" sounds unpleasantly autocratic, whereas "It's like nine o'clock" sounds suitably tentative and non-doctrinaire. "Totally" is another potentially contagious Americanism, as in "Is my husband dead, doctor?" "Totally."

Even though some of the words I have listed have infiltrated the speech of other English-speaking nations, most of them are still a lot more common in the USA than in the UK, and some of them are scarcely to be heard outside the States at all. If the word "awesome" were banned from American speech, airplanes would fall from the skies, cars would lurch wildly off freeways, elevators would shudder to a halt between floors, and goldfish would commit suicide by leaping despairingly from their bowls. Yet other speakers of English use it very little, if at all. The British do not commonly say "meet with," "reach out to," "stay focused," or "your respected college" (which sounds slightly unctuous to non-American ears). They do not zero in, craft a proposal, desire golden hamsters to be empowered, have a hard time understanding something, ask to be given a break, or tackle a situation aggressively, unless by the latter they mean taking a machine gun to it. Using the word "aggressive" to mean admirably robust, a speech habit which does not reflect particularly well on American culture, sounds almost as odd to the British as complimenting someone on being as ugly as sin. The American use of the word "scary" instead of "frightening" or "alarming" sounds childish to British ears, as though one were to talk about one's bottie rather than one's buttocks. To call someone "driven" is a compliment in the States but a criticism in Britain.

"Empower" is a peculiarly American word, and despite being much overused has its virtues. Without really intending to, it challenges the familiar liberal misconception that power is a bad thing. On the contrary, power is an excellent thing, as long as it is exercised by the right people for the right reasons. Only those who have enough of the stuff already can afford to be so disparaging about it. Power is not always oppressive, as some leftists seem to imagine, any more than authority is always to be resisted. There are beneficial forms of power as well as malign ones. There is the authority of those who are seasoned in the fight for justice, as well as the authority that ejects you from a restaurant for not wearing a tie.

Most speakers of British English do not say "a bunch of air," speak of money as the bottom line, or seek closure. "At this time" is not used to mean right now. Things are ascertained, not determined. The British say "It must be," whereas Americans tend to say "It has to be." You can feel comfortable with something in Britain, but nothing like as often as in America. You would not generally say "We feel comfortable using this taxi company," any more than you would ask someone whether they felt comfortable with the idea of being scourged till the blood ran down their thighs. Your actions may influence a situation, but they cannot impact it, just as you can protest against a ruling but not protest it. To do something momentarily in Britain is to do it for a few moments only, not to do it very soon. This is why it sounds curious to British ears to speak of momentarily cutting your head off, or momentarily ploughing your way through *War and Peace*.

Americans say "Excuse me" when they accidentally get in your way, whereas the British say "Sorry." They reserve "Excuse me" for either trying to squeeze past someone, or buttonholing a stranger on the street. One knows one is back in the United Kingdom when everyone is constantly saying "sorry" for no reason whatsoever. When a friend of mine is asked by a waiter what he would like to order, he cannot help starting his answer with the word "sorry," as though he is distraught at putting the restaurant to the trouble of relieving him of his money. If someone slams rudely into you in London, you say "sorry." No doubt the British will soon be apologising for being stabbed in the street.

What you say in Britain when you don't hear what someone says depends on your social class. The working class say "Aye?", the lower middle class "Pardon?", the middle class "Sorry?" and the upper class "What?" Lower-middle-class people whisper furtively in public, the middle classes speak at normal volume, and the upper classes bray. It belongs to upper-class self-assurance to assume that you have the right to say what you like as loudly as you like, rather as noblemen once had the right to hang revolting peasants or deflower their brides on their wedding night. One is thus forced to overhear the conversation of the well-bred, though these days in Britain plenty of people are only too glad to hear what you are saying. Strangers who used to try to conceal the fact that they were eavesdropping on you have stopped pretending and just shamelessly listen in, occasionally with their hand cupped to their ear. No doubt they will soon be asking you irritably to speak up. Similarly, there was a time when the people at the next table to you in a restaurant used to pretend that they were not staring inquisitively at your food when it arrived. Nowadays they are more likely to stroll over to your table and peer open-mouthed over your shoulder. They might even take photographs of your meal on their cell phone and send them to their friends.

Nobody in Britain zeroes in or stays focused. Though they occasionally get excited, the word is less common than it is in the States, where people quite often say things like "It's fun, it's exciting, I love it." Enthusiasm in Britain is regarded as mildly vulgar. In the seventeenth century, it was thought to be responsible for the beheading of a king. This is why the British do not usually say "I love it," unless they are talking about pie and chips or seeing their boss fall down a manhole. Americans, however, are embarrassingly spendthrift in their use of the word "love." One of my children once attended a junior high school in the American Midwest, where the principal would come on the public address system at the end of each school day with a grim list of warnings and prohibitions, rounded off with a cheery "And don't forget—we love ya!" It wouldn't happen at Eton. (The right-wing geography master at the school used to gaze out of the classroom window at the first appearance of a snowflake and sneer to the students "Global warming, huh?") "Love" in British English is a word to be wheeled out only on special occasions, rather like "genitalia," "prosopopoeia," or "you unspeakable little shit." One can contrast this with the wisdom of the American self-help guru Joe Vitale, who recommends increasing one's business by looking over one's mailing list and "loving each name."

All the same, there is much to be admired in the emotional frankness and directness of Americans. At the very least, it saves a lot of tedious conversational spadework, a phrase used by a character in P. G. Wodehouse when he realises that the person to whom he is speaking does not understand the word "pig." At best, it belongs with Americans' warmth and honesty. It is this honesty which leads some Americans to regard the British as devious and hypocritical, even when they are being nothing of the kind. To be reserved is not necessarily to be two-faced. Americans sometimes suspect that the British are being deceitful when they are really just being quiet, or that they are craftily concealing their thoughts when they haven't an idea in their heads.

In Britain, you do not generally buy into an idea. That Americans buy into ideas and proposals all the time suggests just how much the life of the mind is modelled on the stock market. A bathroom in Britain is not a facility, nor is a building a structure. The proud phrase "World's tallest structure" sounds faintly comic to British ears. The British sometimes speak of children as "kids," but they would rarely do so in a newspaper headline or TV news report. This would be almost as inappropriate as the president publicly declaring that China sucks, or a physician talking to you about your ass. The same applies to "guys" or "cops," terms which few British television journalists would use on camera, but which they might employ when it was turned off. The British use the rather beautiful word "children" far more often than Americans do, who tend to prefer the ugly, demeaning monosyllable "kids." It is surprising that a nation so scrupulous about political correctness should be content to regard its offspring as small smelly goats. Perhaps portraits of the Virgin Mary with the child Jesus should be renamed "Madonna and Kid." Clinics could specialise in kid psychology. Wordsworth's line "The Child is Father of the Man" could be rewritten as "The Kid is Old Man of the Guy."

I include "family" in the list of typical American words not because Europeans spring miraculously from their own loins and are ignorant of any such institution, but because the term is more central to American discourse than it is elsewhere. It is used much more often in advertisements and political speeches than it is in Europe. A British politician would not typically refer to "Britain's families," whereas the phrase "America's families" crops up regularly in the States. To mention people's families is among other things to remind them that they have a number of vulnerable young lives dependent on them, and thus should think twice before behaving rashly. Appeals to the family are almost always right-wing. Stalin, a devout moral conservative, spoke with some satisfaction of having millions of little states at his disposal in the Soviet Union, by which he meant millions of families. Today, we might add millions of little consumer units. The British buy and sell houses, while the Americans buy and sell homes. "Home" is a homelier word than "house." You go to someone's house in Britain, but to their home in the United States. "Home" to British ears has vaguely negative connotations. It is a place where you put old people, stray dogs and orphans.

American English can sometimes sound oddly informal to the British, and at other times too straitlaced and well upholstered. The United States is the abode of opaque academic jargon, but also of the raw, racy and in-your-face. It finds it hard to evolve a kind of language which is both easy and elegant. It sometimes suspects, wrongly, that to be clear you have to be plain, and that to be stylish is to be effete. We can appeal to de Tocqueville once more, who notes that American language is clear and dry, "without the slightest ornament," but that it quickly turns pompous and bombastic when its speakers attempt a more poetic style. When this happens, he remarks, Americans can never say anything simply, which is true of their pretentious business or academic jargon today. Bombast, one might claim, is the flipside of an excessive plainness. It is the rhetorical mode of those who are accustomed to unadorned prose.

There can be an alluring courtesy about American speech, along with a rather portentous solemnity. Many years ago, a team of students from Yale arrived in England to debate with a team from Manchester. The Yale captain rose in the debating chamber and announced: "Ladies and gentlemen, I'm from Yale: Y for Youth, A for Ambition, L for Loyalty, E for Enterprise." "Thank Christ he doesn't come from the Massachusetts Institute of Technology," an Englishman at the back was heard to mutter. American English is full of edifying, chivalric, hand-on-heart words like pride, trust, honour, faith, loyalty, service, obligation, responsibility, our brave men and women in uniform, and so on. In some ways, it is the language of top-hatted, frock-coated Victorian England.

So the formal and informal sit cheek by jowl in American English. On the one hand, road signs reading "Wrong Way—Go

Back," "Ped Xing" or "Don't Block the Box" are more startlingly idiomatic than anything one would find in the stiffer-lipped United Kingdom. Perhaps the British could take a leaf out of the U.S. book in this respect and have road signs reading "Bloody Great Pothole Somewhere Up Ahead." (There are, incidentally, some curiously cowardly road signs in Scotland reading "Beware of Sheep.") As far as informality goes, American publishers tend to favour chattily colloquial book titles such as *Phobia: How I Learnt to Conquer My Fear of People Who Have Squeaky Voices and Are Under Five Foot Eight Inches Tall.*

On the other hand, American English can have a rather quaint, earnestly Victorian ring to it, as in "I appreciate your patience, sir, and will make a commitment to you," which was once said to me by an American student. In Britain, this would probably be taken as sardonic. People in Britain do not say "I appreciate it." They simply mutter something shy and unintelligible. Perhaps it was this kind of formal language de Tocqueville had in mind when he remarked that Americans expatiate rather than talk, speaking to you (as Queen Victoria famously complained of Gladstone) as though they are addressing a public meeting. The States may be technologically advanced, but its speech can be charmingly elaborate and old-fashioned. As a country, it is both archaic and avant-garde. Some of its beliefs are only a couple of hundred years old, whereas others date back to the first century AD.

Americans tend to lapse into the present tense when speaking of past events much more than the British do, as in "I'm in the kitchen and there's this tremendous bang and I dive under the table." Perhaps this reflects a present-oriented society. "There's *this* tremendous bang" is also typically American; the

British would probably say "*a* tremendous bang." "He flunked math," or "No determination on that question has been achieved at this moment in time," are almost as foreign-sounding in Glasgow or Brighton as *Sieg Heil* or *la plume de ma tante.* British people use the word "dream," of course, but nowhere is it as current as in the United States, except among psychoanalysts. "My hopes and dreams" trips off the American tongue as glibly as the dreary clichés "at the end of the day" and "over the moon" issue from British lips. "Dream" in anti-idealist Britain is more likely to mean illusion than vision. In America, by contrast, the word comes accompanied by a mistiness of the eyes and the distant sound of swooping violins.

"Miracle" is another term excessively bandied about in the States, a country in which it is hard to fall into a few inches of water and clamber instantly out again without someone branding your survival miraculous. The United States is also crammed with heroes from coast to coast, some of them having attained that title on the slimmest of pretexts, whereas the British are for the most part as embarrassed by heroism as they are by histrionic outbursts of emotion. They would not suppose that it was heroic, as opposed to tragic, to die by having an aircraft slam into your office. Nor are all soldiers who fall in battle heroes. Some of them are, while others are perpetrators of war crimes and should be arraigned rather than applauded. Americans also tend to be rather obsessive about role models, which nobody else on the planet seems to be. It goes with their admiration for the idea of leadership. There are plenty of us who would much rather follow, preferably a long way behind.

If I have included "America" in the list of words more common in the United States than Britain, it is not for the obvious reason that Americans, like anyone else, are bound to mention their country quite a lot. It is rather that they use the word America (as in "Good Morning, America!", "a very fine American," "my fellow Americans," "The American people," "proudly serving America's families since 1953" and so on) a lot more than the Swiss talk about Switzerland or the Greeks about Greece. I once saw a television programme about Peru in which an army officer exhorted his soldiers: "Men, always remember that you are Peruvians." This sounds funny, rather like saying: "Always remember that you are hairdressers," or "Never forget that you are shoplifters," since the word "Peruvian" does not carry any especially exalted implications, at least for non-Peruvians.

The phrase "a very fine American" is revealing in this respect. It is not quite the same as speaking of a very fine Sri Lankan. "America" is a term of approbation, not just a description. It is a moral word as much as a geographical one. The very word "America" implies certain cherished values, so that phrases like "American values" or "a very fine American" are almost tautologies. "A very fine American" is a distinguished example of a noble species, whereas a very fine Sri Lankan is an outstanding individual who happens to come from Sri Lanka. It is suitable that the national symbol of the United States is the eagle. In Wales, it is the leek.

Accents

Americans often speak of the British accent, which is in fact as mythical as the mermaid. There are English, Scottish, Welsh and Northern Irish forms of speech, but no British one. Strictly speaking, even an English accent is something of a misnomer. It generally refers to so-called Standard English, which only a small minority of the English actually speak and so is scarcely much of a standard. Truly genteel people have their own strangulated idiom of Standard English, which sounds as though they are speaking with a hot potato in their mouths. In this kind of speech, "I'm rarely tarred" means not that you are infrequently coated with a sticky black substance, but that you are really tired. Prince Charles speaks in this style, while the BBC speaks regular Standard English (though even this is on the wane). Outside the middle and upper classes, the British tend to speak with the accent of their region. In fact, Standard English was once a regional accent itself.

As far as detecting accents goes, a good many Britons would be able to distinguish between a Texan and a New Yorker, but not many Americans could tell the difference between a Geordie (from north-east England) and a Brummie (from Birmingham). They might also be unaware that a Londoner can find someone from Glasgow almost as unintelligible as he would find a Bulgarian. A Dane and a Norwegian, each speaking his or her own language, might understand each other better.

However indifferently Americans may sometimes speak English, the British can always go one better. "Fortuitously" in Britain has come to mean "fortunately," "refute" is used for "rebut," and to beg a question is to raise one. The British now use the word "literally" when they don't mean it literally at all, as in "I literally fell through the floor with amazement." Anything that is about to happen must be marked by a "potentially," as in "She may potentially be charged with an offence." Things are not done every day, but "on a daily basis."

Abuse

Americans, however, are more concerned than the British by another kind of speech, namely, abusive language. Hawthorne's scarlet letter no longer stands for adultery. What used to be argumentative is now abusive or insensitive. It is insensitive to raise your voice, vigorously dissent, display images of emaciated African children, or criticise the conduct of a nation in the presence of someone who supports it. In a society which finds the negative and discomforting hard to handle, anything which disturbs one's serenity can be nullified by being consigned to the category of abuse. Birds which sing too loudly at dawn are abusive, aggressively violating one's aural spaces. People who wear bright scarlet shirts are being visually abusive. They might even be at risk of being sued, or at least of being forced to buy you a pair of shades. Gutters which drip water on one's head are guilty of abuse, as are pieces of grit that are negligent enough to lodge in one's eye. They, too, may be at risk of being taken to court. Floors which refuse to stop swaying when one is drunk can be indicted for criminal irresponsibility.

To tell someone that their beliefs are a lot of rubbish is most certainly considered insensitive, even though it is an essential part of the democratic process. The idea that one should respect other people's beliefs simply because they are other people's beliefs is plainly absurd. It is like claiming that one should admire the cut of people's trousers simply because they are people's trousers. If my beliefs are arrant nonsense, I expect you to have the decency to tell me so. It would help if you did not call me a slimy little rat in the process, but it is not indispensable. Do those who urge respect for the creed of Rastafarians extend a

similar welcome to the doctrines of the Moonies? Is the belief
that men after death will get to rule their own universe, but
women will not, to be greeted with reverence simply because it
is held by Mormons? Can nothing be said to be plainly ridiculous as long as it is touted by a minority? What about those
American Evangelical sects who are preparing to film the Second Coming, and engage in intricate technical debates about
where best to set up the cameras?

Tolerance does not mean respecting viewpoints simply
because they are viewpoints. It means accepting that ideas
which make you feel sick in your stomach should be granted as
much of a hearing as those that send an erotic tingle down your
spine, provided such views do not put others at risk, and provided you have done your damnedest to argue their advocates
out of their fatuous or obnoxious opinions. Otherwise you are
simply buying your tolerance on the cheap. Dismissing whatever
one finds offensive as "abuse" is a distinctly American brand of
intolerance.

Volume

Americans, unlike Europeans, are generally said to be loud. In
fact, the volume in Europe is gradually turned up as you sink
southwards from Sweden to Sicily. Dockers in Naples and sailors
in Athens can sound as though they are bawling murderous
insults at each other when they are actually just inquiring tenderly after each other's children. In the days when their telephone technology was poor, the Chinese used to bellow so
loudly down the receiver that they could probably have heard

each other without the aid of it. There are also national differences when it comes to noise in general. If some European countries are quieter places than the States, it is partly because the use of sirens and flashing lights by emergency vehicles, except when absolutely necessary, is considered anti-social. It is true that "absolutely necessary" may include dashing back to base, all sirens blaring, when the news comes over the radio that your lunch is getting cold. Generally speaking, however, the air of most European cities is not permanently rent by the shriekings and wailings of the emergency services. On the other hand, British towns are besieged at night by the sound of brawling drunks far more than their law-abiding U.S. counterparts. Many of these places in America are ghost towns after dusk, lacking as they do all notion of a night life. They pay for their tranquillity in the coin of a deep-seated dullness.

Americans can indeed be loud. Most American men have a "Yoo-hoo!" buried somewhere inside them. But the loudness is a matter of timbre as well as volume. There is a particular kind of American voice, common to both men and women, which is peculiarly piercing and resonant, so that whole conversations conducted in normal tones are audible from a couple of hundred yards away without the slightest strain on the speaker's part. People with voices like this might be usefully employed as human foghorns, stationed around the coast to warn shipping of treacherous rocks. They are also, however, especially suited to TV news networks. Whereas European television journalists address their audiences in normal conversational tones, American reporters are clearly selected for the bat-like shrillness or stentorian loudness of their delivery. Even when they are standing in the middle of a tranquil Indiana corn field, they sound as though they are trying to make themselves heard through a tornado. The truth is that they are actually trying to make themselves heard in noisy American living rooms, and that if they fail to grab the viewer's attention, so will the advertisements. In this sense, there is a connection between pitch and the profit motive. One may contrast these tones with the soothing, earnest, measured, concerned, deep-throated voice of U.S. public broadcasting. There is a liberal-Democratic American voice as well as a right-wing Republican one.

Language and the Irish

When it comes to verbal matters, there are particular pitfalls lying in wait for Americans who visit Ireland. Many of them may be unaware that though Northern Ireland is officially part of Britain, it is not part of Great Britain. It is, however, part of the United Kingdom, just to compound the confusion. Many Irish republicans find the term "Northern Ireland" objectionable, since it seems to legitimate the political status quo. They might speak of "the six counties" instead (or the "sick counties," as the Irish novelist Flann O'Brien has it). Some people in Northern Ireland regard themselves as British, some as Irish, and some as both. Some of those who see themselves as British would regard the Irish Catholic population in the North as being as much alien interlopers in their land as Kenyans or Cambodians.

Most of the Irish do not regard themselves as part of the British Isles, since most of Ireland is no longer British. Apart from "these islands," however, there is no convenient phrase to describe the two places as a whole. Since most of Ireland is not part of Britain, it would be both offensive and incorrect in Ireland to refer to Britain as "the mainland," though Northern Unionists would use the phrase. It would be as unacceptable as New Zealanders calling Australia the mainland. For Irish republicans, calling the Northern Irish city of Derry Londonderry would be as heinous an offence as calling Native Americans redskins.

American tourists should know that there is a Northern Ireland but not a southern one. The term "southern Ireland" is rarely used by the Irish themselves, since they regard themselves simply as Irish, and perhaps because it implies acceptance of the partition of the country. (Though Dublin has now in fact officially accepted it.) "Ireland" or "the Irish Republic" will do instead—though to compound the complications, some Irish republicans would reserve the latter phrase for a nation which does not yet exist, namely, an Ireland completely independent of Britain. The Irish Republican Army (IRA) sees itself as deriving its authority from a future it has yet to create. In any case, some bits of so-called southern Ireland are geographically to the north of some bits of Northern Ireland. The preposterous word "Eire" should be avoided at all costs, for reasons too tedious to recount. It is probably best to forget about these geopolitical puzzles and simply enjoy the scenery.

The Irish language, incidentally, is called Irish, not Gaelic, since the latter term covers a whole family of languages. To say you speak Gaelic would be a bit like an Englishman saying he spoke Indo-European. Extensive brain surgery is required in order to learn Irish. The language most Irish people speak is known as Hiberno-English, and includes such imaginative terms of abuse as "gobshite" and "fecking." The latter word, overseas visitors will be surprised to hear, is not a sanitised version of a somewhat stronger oath. The Irish version of that is "fugghan," repeated by some of the population every six seconds or so except during the more solemn parts of the Mass.

There are, then, a number of linguistic and geopolitical traps in Ireland to catch the unwary. But the same could be said of the United States. Why do its inhabitants call themselves Americans? Why are Mexicans and Canadians not Americans as well? Isn't this rather like the Chinese being allowed to call themselves Asians, but not Indians or Koreans? Is a certain land grabbing built into the very way its citizens designate themselves? I was once treated to a fine example of U.S. linguistic imperialism when an American editor changed the phrase *The Times*, which I had written in a reference to the London newspaper of that name, to *The London Times*. My efforts to point out that there is no such periodical were dismally ineffective. According to U.S. journalistic practice, so I was advised, *The Times* of London is indeed called *The London Times*, even though it is not. It is up to the United States to decide what the names of other people's newspapers are. One can imagine other such alterations. "We know your prime minister is actually called David Cameron, but we like to call him Billy Badger." "Your correspondent spent an interesting afternoon in Popesville, known to the natives as Vatican City." "After viewing the Finger, or the Eiffel Tower as the inhabitants quaintly call it, we spent an instructive morning strolling around Main Street, known to the locals as the Champs Elysées."

This is not as improbable as it sounds. The American golfer Bubba Watson once caused an uproar in France by announcing that he had seen "that big tower" (the Eiffel Tower), the "building starting with a L" (the Louvre), and "this arch I drove around in a circle" (the Arc de Triomphe). He later excused his ignorance on the grounds that he "wasn't a history major." Perhaps he had trouble distinguishing history from geography. He also declared that he felt "uncomfortable" (indispensable American word) with being criticised for these *faux pas*.

At a Loss for Words

There is a great tradition of American writing, epitomised in the modern age by the burnished masterpieces of Saul Bellow, in which a luminous poetry is plucked from the prose of everyday life, and the patois of hucksters and dockers invested with epic grandeur. Such writing, at once mundane and magnificent, transcends the commonplace without leaving it behind. It preserves the feel and texture of everyday existence while disclosing a depth within it. Behind this literary heritage, as behind so much in the United States, lies the culture of Puritanism, with its conviction that daily life is the arena of salvation and damnation. The everyday is the place where the most momentous questions are to be confronted. It is a belief that lends itself naturally to the novel.

There have been too many tales of literary decline, too many premature obituary notices for the novel, too much traditionalist nostalgia for a golden age of letters. Even so, it is hard not to feel that the culture of the word has taken something of a nose dive in today's United States. The same is true of Britain, though to a lesser degree. There is a British television show in which panellists engage in superbly witty exchanges and surreal flights of comic fantasy without a single word being scripted. On American TV, by contrast, it is impossible to say "Hey!" or "Wow!" without the aid of an autocue. Hamlet's dying words were "Absent thee from felicity awhile/And in this harsh world draw thy breath in pain/To tell my story. . . . The rest is silence." Steve Jobs's last words were "Oh wow, oh wow, oh wow!" Perhaps he did not do quite as much for human communication as his fans imagine. Some U.S. academics deliver their papers at conferences as though they are translating from the Sanskrit as they go along. Columns in up-market British newspapers can be intricate and inventive, whereas equivalent pieces in the States tend to be sparse, thinly textured and lexically challenged. An editorial in a British newspaper can be a literary *tour de force*, which is hardly ever true across the Atlantic. Some of the most revered national commentators in the United States write a basic, colourless, crudely utilitarian prose. No decent piece of writing simply tells it like it is, without a sensual delight in the way of telling it.

Generally speaking, American students are a delight to teach. Yet they are not always able to voice a coherent English sentence, even at graduate level. Some of them are easy to mistake for Turks or Albanians who have only just arrived in the country, and are still struggling with the language. Only later does one realise that they grew up in Boston. They tend to tie themselves up in great chains of unwieldy syntax, overlain with a liberal layer of jargon. Dishevelled syntax is true of both genders, but jargon is confined largely to the men. This is part of the painful demise of the spoken word in the United States. Another sign of linguistic decline is the existence of an organisation known as Scientology, a name which is in fact a tautology. It means the knowledge of knowledge. Names, however, are not always rigorously logical. It is only quite recently that a London hospital stopped calling itself the Great Ormond Street Hospital for Sick Children, a title which contains one word too many.

Perhaps the real threat to freedom of speech in the United States is not one to freedom but to speech. Perhaps the nation will end up free to say anything it likes while being incapable of saying it. Nor is logical precision a strength of American students. Many of them have had their brains severely addled by an overdose of media. Perhaps they should all have a compulsory first year in which they learn nothing but how to think and speak straight, ridding themselves of the language of texting as a clinic purges its patients of cocaine. Despite all this, no more generous, open-minded and enthusiastic group of students can be found in the world. American students tend to be courteous, responsive, cooperative, eager to acquire ideas and ready to criticise anything whatsoever, not least themselves. They are also the last group of students on the planet who are prepared to speak up in class.

Irony

I once wrote a piece for the *New York Times* that included a few mild touches of irony, only to be informed by a startled journalist on the paper that irony was unacceptable in its columns. One should be as wary of writing for a journal which bans irony as one should for one which seeks to ban immigrants. There are English journals, by contrast, in which the use of irony is almost as compulsory as the use of commas. Pieces can be sent back for being insufficiently insincere.

It is a mistake to think that Americans do not understand irony. Yet though they may respond to it, they rarely initiate it. They also occasionally blunt its edge by too blatantly sarcastic a tone. For a puritan civilisation, irony is too close to lying for comfort. A renowned American philosopher once told me of a discomforting time he had spent at an Oxford High Table. Throughout the entire evening, he had no idea whether a single word that was said to him was meant to be serious or not. "Dammit!" he exploded to me, "I'm an American!" And this was a philosopher for whom irony was a precious moral posture, though he did not seem to appreciate the irony.

One of the gravest moral defects of Americans is that they tend to be straight, honest and plain-speaking. There have been various attempts to cure them of these vices, including the establishment of clinics where they can receive intensive therapy for their distressing tendency to mean what they say. Even with compulsory daily readings of Oscar Wilde, however, it is hard to rid them of the prejudice that there is something admirable about what you see being what you get. ("I live in constant fear of not being misunderstood," Wilde once remarked, a statement it is hard to imagine on the lips of Pat Robertson.) For puritan types, appearances must correspond with realities, the outer present a faithful portrait of the inner, whereas irony involves a skewing of the two. To the puritan mind, appearances are acceptable only if they convey a substantial inner truth. Otherwise they are to be mistrusted as specious and superficial. Hence the familiar American insistence that what matters about a person is what is inside them. It is a claim that sits oddly with a society obsessed with self-presentation. There is no room here for what Lenin called the reality of appearances, no appreciation of just how profound surfaces can be, no rejoicing in forms, masks and signifiers for their own sake. Henry James writes in *The American Scene* of the country's disastrous disregard for appearances. For the Calvinist, a delight in anything for its own sake is sinful. Pleasure must be instrumental to some more worthy goal such as procreation, rather as play on children's TV in the States must be tied to some grimly didactic purpose. It can rarely be an end in itself. The fact that there is no social reality without its admixture of artifice, that truth works in terms of masks and conventions, is fatally overlooked.

The philosopher Wittgenstein once remarked that "A dog cannot lie, but neither can he be sincere," meaning among other things that sincerity is as much something you acquire socially as a large bank balance or a reputation for reclusiveness. Jane Austen knew well enough that to be natural, rather like being ironic, is a form of social behaviour one has to learn. For her, observing the social conventions was a question of respect and consideration for others. No ceremony could be less empty. Nothing is more artificial than a cult of shambling spontaneity. People who are self-consciously blunt, plain and forthright are in the grip of an image of themselves quite as much as people who think they are Elvis Presley or Mother Teresa.

Language for the puritan is at its finest when it clings to the unvarnished facts. This prejudice has given rise in the States to a thousand creative writing classes in which sentences like "And then we rolled into town still hauling the dead mule and Davy said how about some fried eggs and he was still kind of sniggering at the thought of Charlie hollering at that goddam prairie dog and we landed up at Joey's place with the sun still warm on our backs and the coffee was good and strong" are judged superior to anything that overhyped Stratford hack ever managed to pull off. The United States is one of the few places in which stylelessness has become a style, cultivated with all the passion and precision of a Woolf or a Joyce. It is against this current that the likes of Bellow, Toni Morrison and Adrienne Rich are forced to swim.

It was not always thus. Jeffersonian Virginia was renowned for its oratory and rhetoric. The genteel class of New England were praised for what one observer called their "intellectual vigour, exalted morals, classical erudition, and refined taste." Elegance was in high regard. A fluency of speech and manner was thought by some Americans of the period to provide a bulwark against the dangers of demagoguery. There were those, to be sure, who regarded rhetoric as suspect. It was a form of manipulative speech typical of the ruling powers of the Old World, and thus out of place in a genuine democracy. Even so, a nineteenth-century American writer praised "the chaste and classical beauty" of the nation's finest legal scholarship. The lawyer, wrote another commentator of the time, will exhibit "that combination of intellectual power, brilliant but chaste images, pure language, calm self-possession, graceful and modest bearing, indicative of a spirit chastened, enriched, and adorned" by a study of classical civilisation. It is a far cry from Judge Judy.

Henry James thought that America lacked mystery and secrecy, that its landscapes were all foreground, but found just such an air of enigma in Europe. This was not, he considered, by any means wholly to its credit. Civilisations which prize the mannered, devious, playful and oblique generally have aristocratic roots, since it is hard to be mannered, devious and playful while you are drilling a coal seam or dry-cleaning a jacket. And aristocratic social orders, as James was to discover, can be full of suavely concealed brutality. A dash of American directness would do them no harm at all. A culture of irony requires a certain degree of leisure. You need to be privileged enough not to have any pressing need for the plain truth. Facts can be left to factory owners.

Even so, there are times when irony is the only weapon one has at hand. Take, for example, those freakish right-wing Christians in the States who brandish banners reading "God Hates Fags" and gather to rejoice at the funerals of servicemen and women killed in Iraq or Afghanistan. Such people relish nothing more than for some passing liberal to engage them in indignant debate, denouncing their bigotry and homophobia. To do so is surely a grave mistake. Instead, one should ask them why they are such a bunch of liberal wimps. Why are they waving their banners when they could be acting as the Lord's avenging arm by wiping his enemies from the face of the earth? Why don't they actually *do* something for a change, have the courage of their convictions, rather than standing spinelessly around? Why are they such a gutless bunch of whingers?

One of the classic forms of American humour is the gag, which marks its distance from the seriousness of everyday life rather as wearing a baseball cap marks the fact that the American male is on vacation. Wearing a baseball cap signals "I Am Enjoying Myself" even when you are not, rather as a bishop's mitre signals "I Am Holy" even when he is indulging in indecent fantasies beneath it. Humour in this view represents a holiday from reality, rather than a consistent stance towards it.

Nobody is likely to mistake it for the real world. Most gags do not force you to reassess your relationship to reality.

For a certain kind of English patrician, by contrast, irony is less a figure of speech than a way of life. As a highly Europeanised American observes in Henry James's *The Europeans*, "I don't think it's what one does or doesn't do that promotes enjoyment. . . . It is the general way of looking at life." The gentleman's amused, ironic outlook on human existence is a way of engaging with the world while also keeping it languidly at arm's length. It suggests an awareness of different possibilities, one beyond the reach of those who must immerse themselves in the actual in order to survive. The aristocrat can savour a variety of viewpoints because none of them is likely to undermine his own. This is because he has no viewpoint of his own. Opinions are for the plebs. It is not done to be passionate about things. To have a point of view is to be as uncouth and one-sided as a militant trade unionist. It would be a threat to one's *sang froid*, and thus to one's sovereignty. To find the cosmos mildly entertaining has always been a sign of power in Britain. It is the political reality behind Oxford and Cambridge wit. Seriousness is for scientists and shopkeepers.

One of the finest exponents of the English language in the United States today has been the art critic T. J. Clark. Another was the late Christopher Hitchens. Both of them came to the country from England. It can be claimed that to write as well as this, with such tonal subtlety, verbal self-assurance and exquisite play of light and shade, you need a well-established cultural tradition in your bones. In England, that culture has often enough been snobbish, malevolent, and supercilious. The novelist Evelyn Waugh had all of these vices to excess, yet they are also related in complex ways to the splendour of his style.

That permanent house guest of England, Henry James, pressed the nuance and ambiguity of English writing to the point where his prose threatened to disappear up its own intricacies. Among other things, it was a way of putting some daylight between himself and his plain-speaking native land, as was his habit of sucking up to a set of boneheaded English aristocrats. Nothing, not even Communism, could be more anti-American than James's mannered, fastidious, overbred later style, horrified as it would be at the very idea of telling it like it is. Like James, the English upper classes value a certain verbal obliquity. This is because to talk confessionally is considered unsophisticated, and people of this rank would rather be thought wicked than naive. In this, they are at one with the natives of Paris. You would not ask someone like this on first meeting how many children he had, not because it is impertinent but because it is hard for him to return a stylish reply.

The style, they say, is the man. A friend of mine in New York once gave a copy of my *Literary Theory: An Introduction* to a friend of hers, an American woman who belonged to that wretched minority of creatures on the planet who have never heard of me. On handing the book back to my friend, the woman inquired "Is he gay?" No, said my friend. The woman pondered for a moment. "Is he English?" she asked.

Satire

Most Americans are too straight-talking to make effective satirists, though many of them have become resigned to others being satirical at their expense, not least about their ineptness as satirists. Commentators can also be too deferential to power to feel easy about mocking it. It is hard to imagine a U.S. television interviewer putting the same embarrassing question to a squirming politician sixteen or so times over, as a BBC journalist once famously did. As for the Irish, they have about as much respect for their politicians as they do for their paedophiles.

Even when political pundits on American TV engage in rowdy debate, there is usually an unspoken obligation to grin and make up at the end. They must leave the impression that their squabbling is basically good-humoured. Perhaps this is written into their contracts. Political debate, after all, is only entertainment. A touch of polemic is good for the ratings, but too much of it would make viewers feel uncomfortable, a capital American crime. What America calls hard ball is soft ball in Europe. Public debate in the States, at least in the media, is generally more emollient than it is in Europe, keener to emphasise points of consensus, more fearful of outright conflict. The bunch of brawling schoolboys known as the House of Commons would probably be arrested for civil disorder in the USA.

In many a British academic conference, there is blood on the floor by the end of the first afternoon. Exchanges can be barbed, even quietly vicious. Americans, however, will tend to preface their criticisms of your lecture with a courteous reference to "your very fine paper," rather as U.S. politicians who clash with each another on television are often careful to record the respect in which they hold each other's views. There is less mutual boot-licking in Europe. In some ways, this courtesy is a deeply attractive aspect of American culture, even if it is not always best suited to establishing the truth. The genuine niceness of some Americans can be hard to distinguish from a certain blandness.

The difference between radicals and others is that radicals suspect that the truth is generally discreditable. It is thus rarely in the open, and a degree of abrasiveness is required to dig it out. What you see is highly unlikely to be what you get.

Blandness, however, hardly characterizes the nation as a whole. On my first visit to New York, where I had come on the audacious mission of teaching two hundred nuns, I wandered into a gift store, browsed a little and then headed for the door. My exit was blocked by a large man with a drooping moustache who was standing with his back to the door. "Okay, so what ya gonna buy?" he asked. I realised after a moment that this was the proprietor and gave him a feeble, English-upper-class-idiot sort of smile. "Come on, what ya gonna buy for Christsakes?" he repeated menacingly, refusing to shift from the door. It was not until some time later that I realised that this visceral aggression was what some New Yorkers regard as humour. It is certainly a lot preferable to arch banter, self-conscious joshing and Boy Scout heartiness.

Being inept at satire or irony does not of course mean lacking a sense of humour. On the contrary, the United States is marvellously rich in comedy. It represents one of its major contributions to world civilisation. The British are thought to be a humorous bunch, but nothing in their media today can outshine *Seinfeld*, *Family Guy*, *Curb Your Enthusiasm*, *The Office* or the early episodes of *The Simpsons*. The British, however, excel at whimsy, which is less common in the States. Because they value eccentricity, they enjoy a vein of humour which is quaint, fanciful and capricious. Some years ago, there flourished briefly in Britain a Gnomes Liberation Movement, whose project was to abduct ornamental gnomes from people's gardens and return them to their owners on the payment of a ransom of candy. Owners who refused this blackmail would sometimes find their kidnapped gnomes lying decapitated on their doorstops, a sinister rim of red around their severed necks.

There are other instances of such humour. The *Guardian* newspaper usually conceals a spoof in its pages on April Fool's Day, which one year appeared in the "Help Wanted" advertisements. There were job ads such as "Dynamic coordinator required for forward-looking project delivering quality service for supervision of progressive resources redistribution," which turned out on closer inspection to mean nothing at all. It would be hard to imagine a quality U.S. newspaper engaging in this practice. Work in the States is a serious business.

TWO

The Outgoing Spirit

Angels and Demons

There is a kind of American speech which sounds too inflated to Europeans. At its least inspired, American English is a language soggy with superlatives: great, fantastic, awesome, amazing, wonderful, incredible (but not, on the whole, superb, formidable, splendid, or magnificent). One sometimes wonders if there has ever been an American who was not a very wonderful person, with the possible exception of Charles Manson.

The novelist Milan Kundera writes in *The Book of Laughter and Forgetting* of a vision of the world he calls angelic—or, somewhat less politely, "shitless." This way of seeing is full of beams, smiles and high-minded platitudes, averse to all that is dark-tinged, recalcitrant or disagreeable. The angelic march cheerfully forward into an ever rosier future, radiant and wide-eyed, disowning all complexity and ambiguity in their triumphalist self-conviction. Kundera is thinking of the ideological rhetoric of the East European Communist states, which were still alive and kicking at the time he was writing, but the point has a bearing on the world's most powerful capitalist nation as well. To the European mind, high-pitched rhetoric suggests among other things racist rants and ranks of goose-stepping warriors. Americans are in love with spectacle, but in the wake of Nazism, spectacle in Europe can never be quite the same again. Instead, in Britain above all, there is ceremony, which is rather different.

The opposite of the angelic for Kundera, predictably enough, is the demonic, by which he means the language of the cynical and nihilistic, one with too little meaning rather than (like the angelic) one stuffed with sonorous clichés. There is enough demonic discourse in the States to suit anyone's taste, but the fact remains that the official rhetoric of the country (which, one should stress, is far from the discourse of everyday life) is too pious, elevated, hand-on-heart and histrionic for us jaded Europeans. A dash of the demonic would do it no harm. The demonic can be found in the edgy, abrasive, sardonic speech of New York Jews, which is much closer to the Irish than it is to the Midwest. When they hear angelic American speech—"this great country of ours," "let freedom ring forth," and the like—most Europeans simply stare at their shoes and wait for it to stop, as some people do whenever Schoenberg comes on the radio. Many Americans, to be fair, find this kind of language just as excruciating.

European political discourse is much more downbeat. You might get away with a reference to freedom, but certainly not to God. Suggesting that the Almighty has a special affection for your nation would sound as absurd as claiming that he has a special affection for gummy bears. Phrases can be tested for their shitless or angelic quality by seeing whether the opposite would make any sense. The Republican politician Mitt Romney solemnly established a Committee for a Strong and Free America, as opposed to a Committee for an Enfeebled and Enslaved one. ("Strong," incidentally, is a favourite American word.) Angelic discourse goes hand in hand with the high seriousness of the American public sphere. Political life in the States is colourful but earnest. It is hard to imagine a goat, nudist, flamboyant cross-dresser or can of baked beans being put up for political election, as they might be in the United Kingdom. Politics can be a circus, but not exactly a carnival. Michael Moore's attempt to have a ficus plant elected to Congress is a magnificent exception.

Angelic language is too extravagant for British taste. Theatre is a venerable British art, but emotional theatricality is as un-British as sunshine. A British, French or German author might end the preface to his or her book with some rather tight-lipped acknowledgements to friends, colleagues and family. American authors, by contrast, have been known to write roughly as follows: "Finally, I should like to thank my incredible wife Marcia (remember that Caesar salad in Dayton, Ohio!), my three unbelievably beautiful children Dent, Tankard, and Placenta, our wonderful mongoose Brian J. Screwdriver who taught me wisdom, forbearance and compassion, and my totally extraordinary colleagues in the Department of Apocalyptic Studies at Christ Is Coming College . . . " One might claim that where Americans and the British differ most is in sensibility. It is this divergence that their shared language tends to conceal. On one reckoning, however, Americans come out of the comparison rather better. They may overdo emotion, but they are not fearful of it. A surplus of feeling has rarely done as much damage as a deficiency of it.

The Kindness of Americans

There is, then, a positive side to the emotional lavishness of the States, as there is to many an American defect. In fact, de Tocqueville writes that what Europeans tend to see as American vices (restlessness of spirit, an immoderate desire for wealth, an excessive love of independence, and so on) are exactly what makes the nation so resplendently successful, and are thus every bit as serviceable to it as its virtues. Extravagant emotion may be mawkish, but it also reflects a kindliness and generosity of spirit which are among the country's most striking characteristics. Dickens remarks that Americans "are, by nature, frank, brave, cordial, hospitable, and affectionate." He also speaks fondly of their warmth of heart and ardent enthusiasm.

All of these qualities are still present in abundance today. The language of the United States may grate with its gushing superlatives, but it can also simply reflect a wish to be pleasant to others. Many a visitor to America has remarked on the astonishing gap between its politics and its people. The latter are for the most part far more congenial than the former. Republics are supposed to be places in which the people and the government are at one, which is thankfully not the case with the republic of America. That the citizens of the country have managed by and large to preserve their neighbourliness, kindliness and largeness of spirit in one of the most acquisitive, ferociously competitive civilisations on God's earth is a remarkable tribute to their innate decency. This may be something of a backhanded compliment, like congratulating someone on winning the title of World's Greatest Bore five times in a row, but it is a compliment nonetheless.

Americans continue to be on the whole an easy, outgoing people. If two of them find themselves together in an elevator, they will usually acknowledge each other's presence with a friendly word. People who speak to you in British elevators are generally regarded as dangerous lunatics who should not be favoured with a reply, since this will only spur them to further outbursts of insanity. If they persist in their offensive attempts to be friendly, one can always press the emergency bell and have them carted away by security. The British are much taken by what one might call the argument from the floodgates. Once you allow one stranger to murmur a cordial remark to you about how the cricket is going, you are in imminent danger of being besieged by great herds of wild-eyed, shaggy-haired men and women who will try to talk to you about everything from the structure of the atom to the collapse of the Holy Roman Empire. Strangers who smile at you in public will always end up demanding to live in your spare room. They will try to kidnap your children, or offload a demented elderly relative on you. It is best to keep yourself to yourself.

Keeping yourself to yourself, however, is not the guarantee of a quiet life that it once was. Whenever those suspected of terrorism are arrested these days, their neighbours almost always remark that they struck them as quiet, polite, respectable-looking people who never failed to give them the time of day, but who kept to themselves. People like this should be instantly reported to the police. Men who are completely covered in hair, brandish Kalashnikovs and speak some strange gibberish are entirely harmless.

Is American friendliness genuine or superficial? There is a case for claiming that it is both. There is certainly a good deal of automated pleasantness, compulsive cheeriness and manufactured bonhomie. There are times when you are not really allowed to feel down in the mouth or enjoy being on your own. Solitariness is seen as anti-social. Americans can often strike one as over-socialised, too frenetically eager to please, too anxious to make an impression in a country where impressions count for more than they should. This, however, is far from the whole story. When I stroll across an American campus, I sometimes pass a young man I don't know, and who doesn't know me, who murmurs, "How ya doin', sir?" This would never happen in Europe. It may be something of a conditioned reflex, but it is an undeniably charming one. There is an agreeableness about many Americans which is less obvious in the case of some Europeans. With them, you may have to dig a little to discover it. In Americans it tends to be more readily accessible, like most other things about them.

Not all Americans, admittedly, are quite as affable as the young men I occasionally bump into on campus. A survey showed that people in Rio touch each other an average of 180 times when drinking coffee together, but only 40 times in New York. Perhaps this is because some Americans believe that touching anything, even their toddlers, is a sure way to contract bubonic plague. There are U.S. citizens who would clearly feel happier spending their lives cocooned in a plastic bag, though some of them might fear that this, too, could result in some loathsome infection. Even if New Yorkers touch each other sparingly, however, the inhabitants of the United States are by and large a more friendly, helpful bunch than the citizens of many a European nation. If you stop on the sidewalk with a map in your hands, they will quite often step up and ask if you need directions.

This tends to happen much less in Europe. In any case, in Britain at least, the art of giving directions on the street is rapidly dying, along with clog dancing and tapestry weaving, as people mistake left for right, omit vital pieces of information, grossly underestimate distances in order to raise your spirits, forget about one-way traffic systems, and take local knowledge complacently for granted. Perhaps the art fares better in the United States. Some of the Irish enjoy turning their road signs around in order to confuse visitors. It is possible for tourists to travel in circles for many hours in the Irish countryside, given the mischievous tendencies of the natives.

The British tend to be suspicious of instant friendliness. There are posters on garbage cans in O'Hare Airport in Chicago that read "We're Glad To See You!" No they're not. They don't even know who I am. How do they know I'm here? Glad to see me personally, or just glad to see anybody? Who exactly is glad to see me? The mayor, the airport authorities, the garbage can manufacturers, or the entire population of the city? How do they know I don't have a test-tube full of lethal germs in my suitcase, or a collapsible nuclear weapon? What if I have come to sell heroin to their teenagers?

Such are the churlish reflections of a visitor from the United Kingdom.

Openness and Obliquity

"I know of no other country," writes de Tocqueville, "where love of money has such a grip on men's hearts." In Ireland, a store will probably let you off a few cents if you find yourself short. It is not certain that this would happen in New York. Irish builders also tend to place coins in the foundations of houses for good luck. An American friend to whom I mentioned this custom was adamant that it would never happen in the United States. It was the waste, not the superstition, he thought was the problem. Perhaps American suburbs would resound at night with the sound of people frantically digging up their neighbours' foundations. There is an enormous amount of generosity in the States, but not much of it extends to the financial sphere.

Even so, being so brashly explicit about money is part of America's openness. In Britain, the oldest capitalist nation in the world, it is not done to discuss the stuff too often or too loudly, whereas one knows one is back in the United States when everyone at the hotel breakfast seems to be talking about dollars. The British can be coyly euphemistic about what Americans candidly call the bottom line. British universities "appoint" their academic staff rather than "hiring" them. One hires plumbers, not professors. (There are those of us who find it gratifying, by the way, that another word for "godly" in early Puritan America was "professor.")

Perhaps one origin of this evasiveness is that aristocrats traditionally had so much money that they did not need to think about it, and so did not need to talk about it either. This is also true of Henry James's fabulously wealthy characters. True gentility means having only the vaguest idea of where your income comes from, as true innocence means not knowing where babies come from. The middle classes make money, and are thus permanently preoccupied with it, while the gentry spend it, and thus do not need to harp on it so much. American talk about dollars may sometimes be brash, but at least is not conducted behind one's hand, as though one is conspiring with a hit man to do away with one's spouse. Old-fashioned Britons talk about money as discreetly as they do about sex. You do not discuss it loudly, any more than you tell a passing stranger about your erectile dysfunction.

There is a similar reticence about the British brand of English. I was once a Fellow of an Oxford college of which the Warden (Principal) was the legendary wit and *bon viveur* Sir Maurice Bowra. It was this patrician rogue who, when invited to the wedding of a glamorous young pair, is said to have remarked, "Lovely couple, slept with them both." Though famously gay, he once rather grudgingly contemplated marriage, and on being asked why he had chosen a rather plain woman with whom to tie the knot, replied breezily, "Ah well, buggers can't be choosers."

Bowra's most superlative term of praise was "far from bad," which is technically known as litotes. In Americanese, this would be the equivalent of "wonderful" preceded by three or four "verys." Shakespeare was far from bad, so was Châteauneuf-du-Pape, and so was lying naked on the banks of the river Isis in full, shameless view of passing boaters. One suspects that in his more pious moments, which were admittedly somewhat rare, Bowra thought that God was far from bad as well. Homer was "quite a clever fellow," while the more melancholic of the nineteenth-century novelists were "the gloomy boys." Botticelli was "not at all a disgrace," though some of the more flamboyant Romantic poets "laid it on a bit thick." Malt whisky, J. S. Bach and ravishingly handsome male undergraduates "could be worse." "Not a little boring" meant mind-numbingly monotonous.

If the British upper classes hold that it is not good form to gush, it is because emotion is seen a form of weakness, and to display such weakness before one's social inferiors or colonial subjects is to risk a bullet through the brain. Emotional constipation can save your life. Those who do not have their tender feelings beaten out of them at school may be subjected to a more lethal kind of beating in the long run. Understatement thus has political roots. It can sometimes be pressed to bizarre extremes. A few years ago, an Englishman who happened to be in Japan when the country was struck by an earthquake, tsunami, large-scale fires and a threat of nuclear meltdown, was asked about the situation on BBC television. "Well," he replied, "it's not very nice and I rather wish it hadn't happened." "Not very nice" is British for "unbelievably awful." When an American is asked how she is, she might reply, "Pretty good." A typical British or Irish response would be, "Not too bad." Or alternatively, "Can't grumble," a statement which has never actually prevented the British from grumbling. It would take a collision with a comet to do that.

Amping Up, Playing Down

The American impulse is to amplify, while the British habit is to diminish. When thanked, an American might say, "It's my pleasure," "You're very welcome" or, "You bet," whereas the British, who tend naturally to the negative and low-profiled, tend to murmur, "Don't mention it," "Not at all," "No problem," or even the hideous "No probs." In an unintended put-down, they imply that they have done nothing worth being thanked for—that being helpful to you does not count as an event, and that your gratitude is therefore both superfluous and embarrassing.

"It can't do any harm" in British English usually means that it is precious beyond words. The British, unlike Americans, speak of "popping" in and out of places. To "pop" into a store is to be there so briefly as not really to be there at all. It is a very British kind of self-effacement. There is never a catastrophe in the United Kingdom, just "a bit of a problem." Neither, as we shall see later, are there any catastrophes in the United States, though for rather different reasons. Instead, they are known as "challenges." It sounds so much less catastrophic. The instinct to play down is as common among the Irish as the British. An Irish acquaintance once told me that he was doing fine, except for "a touch of cancer."

One thing one is supposed to play down in Britain is one's offspring. It is generally considered distasteful to praise one's own children, which is less true in the United States. There are dubious as well as admirable motives for this reticence. The British do not praise their own children rather as they would not boast about their farmhouse in Provence, which implies that they regard their children as counting among their possessions. But at least it means that nobody would sport a notice in the back of their car reading "My Child is on the Honor Roll," as some Americans do. More satirically-minded Britons might display notices reading "My Child is a Hooker" or "I Married an Incurable Alcoholic," but "My Child is on the Honor Roll" is desperately, distinctively American. If you were caught making this kind of pathetic boast in Britain or Ireland, you would probably need to emigrate immediately, or at least have emergency cosmetic surgery to disguise your appearance. (Speaking of signs in cars, an effective way of alarming your neighbours if you live in an up-market suburb called, say, Sandyfield, is to drive around with a poster in the back window of your vehicle reading "Say No to Sandyfield Sewage Plant." If you are looking to buy a cheaper house in the area or dispose of some particularly annoying neighbours, this should do the trick.)

When I hear Americans proudly recounting their children's achievements, I make a point of telling them that I am training up my small daughter to be a pickpocket, and hope she will be adept enough at the trade to avoid joining her three elder brothers in jail. There are, however, plenty of Americans who share this distaste for drooling in public over their offspring. The positive side of such praise is that Americans are not afraid to encourage their children and boost their self-assurance. By and large, they are a supportive people. In working-class Britain, at least when I was growing up there, praising one's children was thought to make them soft, and thus unfit for the tough life that lay ahead of them. It was the kind of soppy thing posh people did.

The Irish are particularly allergic to boasting, and tend to downplay their attainments. Until recently, Ireland was a fairly impoverished place, so that mentioning your villa in Umbria would have been thought tasteless when others were struggling to survive. It is because other people might be short of food that it is customary in Ireland even today to refuse the offer of a meal or even a cup of tea, and then be persuaded to accept. Truly heroic citizens might even refuse the offer of a Guinness. Britain, by contrast, has a history of affluence; but much of that wealth was bound up with its imperial power, and the nation's ruling class was not slow to recognise that power is likely to produce a backlash if exercised too haughtily. This did not stop the British from torturing and massacring their colonial subjects from time to time, but they did so in a modest, unassuming kind of way, as though they were offering them a much-sought-after service.

Among the more emotionally constipated of Britons is the Duke of Edinburgh, who was once asked in the course of a television interview how he felt about having had to abandon a promising naval career to spend the rest of his days walking two paces behind his wife. "Feel about it?" barked the Duke. "I don't go around psychoanalysing myself, you know." It is not quite the response one would expect from a guest on *Oprah*. Introspection for the Duke is a form of illness. Aristocrats like him regard the whole notion of an inner life as a shameless middle-class self-indulgence. Rather than morbidly picking over your finer feelings, you just get on with things. The positive side of this ethic is a rather stiff kind of selflessness. The point is to be of service to others, not to lie around brooding and whining. The negative side is that since the Duke of Edinburgh seems to have about as much inner life as a fruit bat, courteously suppressing it is unlikely to prove much of a problem for him. Americans may hype their emotions, but at least they do not regard them as something to be kept under wraps, like a history of incest or a lunatic uncle.

Emotional reticence is hardly a quality of the U.S. media. In fact, Americans might find themselves astonished at the untheatrical behaviour of Scandinavian TV weather forecasters, who when the camera alights upon them are sometimes to be found with their heads buried shyly in their wall maps. They look as though they would prefer to be anywhere but in front of the public, and mutter their script as though they are reluctantly disclosing some dreadful news, which sometimes they are. No self-conscious joshing, heavy-handed humour or cavort-

ing around for them. British TV weather forecasters, by contrast, tend to have an irritatingly cheerful bedside manner.
They predict that the rain might not carry on for quite the
whole of the summer in the tones of a doctor trying to console
you with the news that the tumour is so far confined to only
one of your kidneys.

Sentimentality

Overseas observers often feel that there is a compulsion in the
States to get everything instantly out in the open. No doubt
there is a streak of puritan confessionalism in this habit. But it
is also part of the emotional forthrightness of Americans, in
contrast to the shyness of the British. Other nations sometimes
regard Americans as lacking in complex inner depths, which is
of course a mistake. But the mistake is a significant one. It is not
that Americans exist only on the surface, but that their surface
is where their depths are supposed to be. They seem to have a
more untroubled passage between inner and outer, a greater fluency in translating the one into the other, than Scots or Swedes.
Puritans may find spectacle and razzmatazz distasteful, but this is
not because these things are on the surface. It is because they
are surfaces which fail to manifest any depths.

The shy and socially awkward, who are plagued by a gap
between their internal and external worlds, probably fare less
well in the United States than they do in, say, Ulster or Malay-
sia. Since the easy expressiveness of Americans is a great aid to
social intercourse, it is mostly a virtue. The country values honesty, directness and spontaneity, which are not quite so high on

Europe's list of moral priorities. They are virtues to which Europeans tip their hats but fail to get excited about. At the same time, honesty and directness can involve the tiresome assumption that keeping things to yourself is morbid and unsociable. One should share one's emotions as one should share one's cookies. In a country which dislikes the idea of living in a house which is attached to someone else's, one's inner space is constantly at stake in the public sphere. In this view, whatever is unexpressed has no real existence. What is inside you is valid only if it is externalised. This is why foreign visitors to the United States can be astonished by how quickly two of its inhabitants can progress from meeting each other for the first time to exchanging steamy details of their sex lives.

It is partly because their feelings are more out in the open that Americans are more sentimental than the British. It is acceptable for them to indulge their emotions in public with a certain theatrical touch, which is less true of their transatlantic cousins. Almost all Oscars received by American actors need a thorough rub-down with a towel by the time they leave the stage. The British are sentimental about animals but not much else, while the Irish are scarcely sentimental at all. Perhaps the harshness of their history plays a part in this tough-mindedness. Irish children are notably more mature than British or American ones. Generally speaking, the Irish do not suppress emotion like the British, but they do not wallow in it either. European politicians are rarely to be found moist-eyed and broken-voiced, with a catch in the breath and a lump in the throat. Some of them are more likely to be found hurling each other across the debating chamber. American politicians, by contrast, are occasionally to be found sobbing in public, as are American judges, bishops, police chiefs, newscasters, and business executives. This is partly because American feelings are near the surface, but also because in the case of politicians, crying in public can be something of a vote-catcher.

Americans like their leaders to be human, a quality which one demonstrates by sobbing or saying something folksy. Being a republic means demanding a government which is in touch with everyday emotion. Americans tend to be suspicious of the aloof, clinical and impersonal. This is why U.S. popular culture almost always portrays crazed scientists, invading aliens and demonic psychopaths as speaking in sinisterly robotic tones. The nation is instinctively humanistic. Many American movies are about the conflict between an anonymous political or technological order and the rugged, warm-blooded individual. The opposition is in fact deceptive. Historically speaking, it was rugged individualism which gave rise to technocratic systems indifferent to human feeling.

Sentimentality and the Family

Sentimentalists tend to believe that the more emotion you display, the more human you are, but the reverse can be the case. I have seen concentration camp survivors in Germany reduce an American audience to tears with an account of their experience, while remaining impassive and level-voiced themselves. The idea that emotion is an adequate response to such horrors is absurd. They lie in a region as far beyond sentiment as the theory of relativity. Those who can sob and wail are the lucky ones. It may be that some American business types and politicians are

sentimental because sentimentality is the emotional mode of
those unaccustomed to genuine feeling. Rather as broad humour
is the only kind of comedy appreciated by the humourless, so
stagey, broad-brush emotion is the speciality of those who are not
often called upon to cope with the subtle motions of the heart.

"Family," as I noted earlier, is a mantra-like American word,
guaranteed to evoke a flow of profit and a flood of warm feeling.
To find this domestic piety in such a robustly Christian nation is
odd, since the New Testament displays a marked hostility to the
family. Jesus, Mary and Joseph are a curious parody of one. As a
child, Jesus wanders off to teach in the Temple, making it clear
to his distraught parents that his public mission takes prece-
dence over his domestic affections. He is careful to point out
that his apparent father is not his real one. His parents do not
seem to be among his immediate comrades, though his mother
shows up at his execution and his brother James ran the church
in Jerusalem (he, too, was later to be executed). When a woman
in the crowd calls out a blessing on the womb that bore Jesus
and the breasts that suckled him, he responds with an acerbic
put-down.

At one point, his family members want a word in his ear
while he is on public business, but Jesus tells them peremptorily
to wait. A few of his relatives even try to lay violent hands on
him, claiming that he is "beside himself." Perhaps they regarded
him as a dreadful embarrassment, hardly an unusual attitude
among family members. Having a family himself would simply
have interfered with his mission. It had nothing to do with
hostility to sex. His commitment was to humanity as a whole,
not to his uncles and aunts. A prospective disciple who asks to
say goodbye to his family before joining Jesus's movement

receives the rough edge of his tongue. Another who asks to be allowed to bury his father before joining up is abruptly advised to let the dead bury their dead. The phrase would no doubt have horrified the Jews around Jesus, who regarded burying the dead as a sacred duty. It might well have sounded to them like a moral obscenity.

Jesus has come, he declares, to tear family members one from the other and set them at each other's throats. A follower of his, he insists, must hate his parents. Some of his disciples today might find this the least arduous of his commandments. If they had been around at the time, advertisers and politicians would have fallen over themselves to shut him up. As it is, the Roman state did it for them, probably at the bidding of a badly rattled colonial ruling elite. Jesus's attitude to the family is good neither for business nor political stability. The American cult of the family is part of the country's religious legacy. Domestic bliss is a key feature of puritan ideology. It is not at all central to the New Testament.

It is also strange to find American Christians so grimly pre-occupied with sex, since there is almost nothing on the subject in the New Testament. One of Jesus's most loyal comrades seems to have been a prostitute, and he himself shows tenderness to a woman from Samaria with a disreputable sexual history. Since Samarians counted as fairly low-life figures among the Jews, the fact that he has dealings with her at all is pretty remarkable. He does not rebuke the woman for her exotic sexual career, but offers her the waters of eternal life, which she gratefully accepts. In general, the New Testament is fairly relaxed about sexuality. This is one of the many ways in which its adherents have betrayed it.

The Unromantic Irish

One can contrast American cosiness about the family with certain traditional domestic attitudes in Ireland. In the nineteenth century, there was little romantic or sentimental about Irish domestic arrangements. American families are important among other things because they provide an emotional refuge from a harsh public world. The more cutthroat and anonymous social life becomes, the more one may expect a cult of domestic affections. In traditional Ireland, by contrast, the domestic unit was locked directly into the socio-economic world. This was known as the family farm. Relationships between family members were governed among other things by economic necessity. Marriage was more a matter of dowries and matchmakers than candle-lit dinners or erotic love. Many of the Irish were lucky to get a dinner at all, candle-lit or otherwise. Fine feelings were for those who could afford them. Sexual reproduction was geared to producing children who would work on the land, as well as provide for their parents in their old age. Celibacy might be enforced on those children who did not inherit the farm. Otherwise they might be compelled to emigrate, or become priests or nuns. Dividing a small farm between too many family members raised the spectre of hardship and even famine.

Visitors to Ireland should remember that though we are all Irish in the eyes of God, the Almighty designed the Irish nation with a specific purpose in mind, namely, as a place for other people to feel romantic about. The Irish are adept at exploiting this role, though they do not feel in the least romantic about themselves and would not be caught dead wearing an Aran sweater or drinking Irish coffee. In fact, the country was recently thrown into blind panic by a malicious rumour that Irish pubs might actually be coming to Ireland. The Irish drink Guinness, of course, but Guinness is not really Irish any longer. The brewery is owned by an international corporation. A number of things that seem to be Irish, such as Irish stew or the founding of Dublin, are not Irish at all. The Irish might, however, engage in such activities as singing "Danny Boy" or saying "Begorrah" (a word which nobody in Ireland has ever been known to utter) simply to please the tourists, rather as lunatics in eighteenth-century London would froth at the mouth and slash at their wrists when visitors came to view them, only to resume their usual demure demeanour once they had gone.

It should be said, incidentally, that one key difference between the Irish and the British is that on the whole the Irish like Americans, whereas generally speaking the English do not. Ireland's affection for the United States is hardly surprising, given the loyal support the country has shown its people over the centuries. In the years after the Great Famine, whole villages in the west of Ireland would have sunk without trace had it not been for the New York Police Department. It was the money its Irish officers sent back home which kept them afloat. The distance from Dublin to Boston is in many ways shorter than that from Dublin to London. Flying to the aid of a downtrodden, semi-destitute country stands as one of the United States's great historic achievements, along with Emily Dickinson and magnificent bacon. (These, however, are to be weighed against its lamentable ignorance of the teapot, which is largely a consequence of never having owned India.) There are aspects of Northern Irish culture (golf, snooker, huge meals, guns, obesity, theme parks, violence, paramilitaries, puritan values, Evangelical fervour) which closely resemble parts of the States. Most U.S. presidents with Irish backgrounds have been from Ulster, the northerly part of the nation.

Innocence and Experience

It is because they are so outgoing that Americans can seem so innocent. However much experience they accumulate, there can still be a freshness and directness about them which seems deeply non-European. Whatever great stacks of human life they already have under their belts, they always seem eager for more, and we associate eagerness with the innocent rather than with the jaded and overbred. It is not, of course, that all Americans really are innocent, any more than all Europeans are devious and decadent. It is rather that straightness and openness are childlike qualities, and childhood and innocence, despite the best efforts of Sigmund Freud, are still thought to be closely allied. Being crafty and deceptive are complex social practices that children have yet to pick up. The day when a child learns to dissemble marks a milestone in its progress towards adulthood, though it would seem strange to celebrate it with a visit to the circus.

Striving to recapture a lost innocence is a staple theme of American culture. Perhaps all civilisations are nostalgic for Eden, but America has more reason for this hankering than most. It has never lost its sense that there is something synthetic and unreal about civilisation. Regaining the happy garden was a constant preoccupation of the early Puritans. There is, however, a paradox about trying to recapture lost innocence, not least in literature.

To write about childlike innocence is inevitably to betray it, since there is no writing in paradise. Language is the sign of a fallen adult world. It signifies that you have been cast out of the happy garden, and does so in the very act of trying to scramble back into it. You cannot get behind language in language. The child's innocence is not meaningful to the child itself, so that trying to retrieve it is less like trying to unearth a buried state of being than like trying to remember what happened last night when you were leglessly drunk. The reason this is so hard is that the brain was probably not laying down memory traces at the time, so there is really nothing to recall. Just the same is true of the child's spontaneity and lack of self-consciousness.

America's love affair with innocence thus involves a degree of self-deception. It also involves an erasure of history. History is guilt, which is one reason why children, who do not languish under the burden of time, seem so guileless. For adults to recreate this condition means continually wiping out their history and treating every moment as though it were miraculously new. In a well-worn American phrase, it is a matter of being born again, though this particular rebirth has to happen all the time. The only way you can recapture the innocence of the child, who is out of time, is to move so fast that you live in a perpetual present. As Henry James comments in an essay on Hawthorne, "A large juvenility is stamped upon the face of things [in America], and in the vividness of the present, the past, which dies so young and had time to produce so little, attracts but scant attention." You can try to outwit time by moving at such speed that every moment is discarded almost before it is done. The trick is to keep cutting the present off from the past. In this way, you can try to deny the fact that the past is what we are made of, and that there would be no present without it. One of the several problems with this way of living is that it is not clear how what is reborn every moment can be said to be you. Personal identity involves a degree of continuity.

We are speaking here of the time of capitalist endeavour, in which whatever is not here and now is dead and done with. History is just so much junk to be jettisoned. It obtrudes its ungainly bulk between the self and the real. Yet it is hard to deny that you can also learn from the past about how to succeed in the present. The ideal condition, then, is to reap the benefits of experience without being wrinkled and withered by it, so that you can remain eternally fresh. Or, as they might say on Wall Street, to have a sizeable store of accumulated capital behind you, but in a way which leaves your hands absolutely free to buy, sell and invest in the present. In the end, however, it is impossible to absorb one's past and shuck it off at the same time. America has a hunger for experience coupled with a desire to abolish it and start again from scratch. It must simply live with this contradiction as best it can.

Henry James in *The American Scene* sees certain houses in New York as proclaiming that they do not care in the least what becomes of them once they have served their purpose. They are as indifferent to the future as they are to the past, since neither stretch of time has any immediacy about it. Yet since each present moment is already melting into the future, there is no such thing as a perpetual present. Nothing is here and now. In any case, this whole conception of time forgets that the past contains precious resources for the present and future. Nations which have nothing to live by but their contemporary experience are poor indeed. To liquidate the past is to help sabotage a finer future. This is one reason why the association between progress and prosperity can be so deceitful.

Eden, then, is something of a con-trick, as it turns out to be in Dickens's *Martin Chuzzlewit*. The hopeful young Martin, arrived in America to make his fortune, is shown the blueprint of a noble city called Eden which is being raised in the wilderness. The plan shows the settlement to be full of banks, churches, factories, hotels and cathedrals, some of which are still to be completed. Since Martin is an architect, he spends his last few dollars in buying into the scheme, and sets off in pursuit of this utopia. It turns out to be a cluster of rotten wooden huts set in a fetid swamp. For the Dickens of this novel, though not for the Dickens of *American Notes*, America itself is a fraud, full of pious hot air and long-winded rhetoric, populated by braggarts and snake-oil salesmen who rave about freedom yet are driven by greed.

In Praise of American Tourists

Americans tend to be open to experience, and among some of them this takes the form of an eagerness to see the world. It is true that American tourists may not always be mathematically certain of what building they are standing in front of, or even at times what country they are in; but they will explore the dullest landmarks, listen attentively to the most tedious of guides, and labour their way up and down the most unforgiving flights of stairs. Their energy is extraordinary, as is their willingness to listen and learn. The natural American tendency is to say yes to things, whereas the natural British tendency is to be cautious. If

visitors from Oregon and Omaha do not always grasp the intricacies of Roman Britain or the English Civil War, it is not for
want of trying. They are a tourist guide's delight. They tend to
be endearingly respectful of foreign customs, and touchingly
afraid of giving offence.

A lot of Britons would not travel abroad at all were it not for
its superior climate. Since the Almighty has chosen in his
unwisdom to make abroad hot and home bloody freezing, they
have no option but to abandon the country from time to time
for a foreign beach (though not usually for a foreign city). This
kind of British tourist is like someone who is compelled to wade
through a snake-ridden swamp in search of a precious jewel.
Some of the British who stay at home are never happier than
when they are poking around in castles, ruins, antique shops,
medieval villages, pottery studios, model railways, rare booksell-
ers, stately homes, tea shops, craft shops and above all, gardens.
The English love gardens so much that it is a wonder they have
not begun to sprout. Gardens represent a dim race memory of
their pre-industrial ancestors. All Englishmen and women are
peasants at heart.

Some Americans are so keen to see the world that they stay
overseas for years on end, usually with a few tanks and helicop-
ters to keep them company. There are also a great many U.S.
citizens who would not turn a hair if New Zealand were to sink
overnight beneath the waves, or who are reluctant to set foot in
Yorkshire for fear of encountering hordes of spear-waving can-
nibals. For these people, abroad is a place where there may be
cobras or Communists, where you cannot lay your hands on a
decent cheeseburger, and where nobody flosses their teeth or
knows what a slam dunk is. What they forget is that the United

States has considerately exported much of its own culture abroad, so that its citizens can feel thoroughly at home there. These days you can probably get a decent cheeseburger on top of Mount Etna. At the end of the movie 2001, a space traveller arrives on a distant planet to find that the aliens have thoughtfully rearranged its appearance in order to make him feel at home. The United States has been doing this on its own planet for many years.

The American tourist's spirit of adventure seems unquenchable. Americans seem to have mental and physical resources quite beyond the shrunken capacities of Europeans. They will drive for days on end, for example, whereas the British need to stop every ten miles to picnic, throw up, exercise the dog or stroll aimlessly around. The fact that there is hardly anywhere in Britain to picnic does nothing to quench the picnicking zeal of its inhabitants. It would not occur to many Americans abroad not to experience as much as possible, whereas an Irish friend of mine once spent three weeks in Paris, a city he had never visited previously, without once leaving his hotel room. His general attitude to abroad was that once you had seen one bit of it, you had seen the lot. Cynics are those who feel much the same about humanity.

Despite America's self-involvement, then, one should recall the insatiable curiosity about the rest of the world that so many of its citizens reveal. It is a desire which drives them to every nook and cranny of the globe, from Moroccan villages to Indonesian temples. This thirst for experience, so characteristic of American culture, shows up well when contrasted with British inertia. A good many of the British do not approve of abroad, whereas some Americans cannot get enough of it.

Nor is it true, as the stereotype has it, that they throw their weight around when they arrive in foreign parts. Far from being loud-mouthed and domineering, some Americans in Europe are more likely to smart under the sense that the natives regard them as flashy and dim-witted. They are sometimes quite right to suspect so. By and large, Americans abroad are a remarkably civil, courteous bunch, which is more than can be said for spewing, scrimmaging British football fans on the rampage in France or Italy. One might point out, however, that some of this spewing and scrimmaging springs from a curious embarrassment on the part of British working-class youths who feel culturally out of their depth away from home, and who react by smashing the place up, rather like a child who is out of control because he has lost his coordinates. Britain, too, is a notoriously insular nation. There are many senses in which it can rival the States in this respect. Ireland is smaller than Britain but much less insular, not least since it never had an empire. The most inward-looking nations are usually those with their gunboats in everyone else's harbours. The Irish also needed to emigrate. For a long time, there have been many more millions of them living outside the country than in it.

The good news for Americans is that most of the world does not regard them as arrogant and thick-headed, though once upon a time it did. American military personnel stationed in Britain during the Second World War were handed a leaflet advising them that the natives expected them to "swank" (brag), and warning them not to. The bad news is that a lot of people see Americans not as thick-headed braggarts but as uncultivated ignoramuses. Ignorance is not the same as lack of intelligence. European attitudes to the United States typically mix a degree of admiration for its inventiveness and never-say-die spirit with a mildly patronising contempt for its culture. Many a formidable power has been both feared and mocked, and the United States is no exception. On the whole, ruling powers have been more tolerated than admired.

On American Loquacity

Americans are unflaggingly active, curious and loquacious. British academics who are asked what they are working on will tend to reply dismissively: "Oh, Gothic, vampires, that sort of thing." They seem no more eager to discuss their research than they are to discuss their haemorrhoids. This is because it is thought bad form to jaw on about oneself and one's work. I spent twenty years in an Oxford college without once hearing my colleagues discuss their work with each other in more than the most cursory way. It is also because the British are modest, and have much to be modest about. If you ask an American academic what he or she is working on, however, you should be sure to equip yourself with a folding chair, a flask of coffee and a thick wedge of sandwiches, since you are still likely to be there three hours later. It is not that Americans are immodest, simply enthusiastic. If you are trying to pick your way through the traffic on Fifth Avenue with an American graduate student at your side, he is bound to ask you what you think about hermeneutical phenomenology just as a taxi is about to toss both of you over its roof.

Behind this British reticence lurks the cult of amateurism, so deeply alien to the United States. One of Henry James's American characters is unclear what the word "amateur" means, but suspects that it may be a European term for a broker or grain exporter. People who hold forth about their work are professionals, and professionals are not really gentlemen. Gentlemen leave earnestness to pastors and specialist knowledge to their chefs. The phrase "to talk shop" suggests that technical discussions are the province of tailors and barbers. Gentlemen are formidably cultivated, but they acquire their cultivation in a careless, offhand, unlaborious way, as you might acquire a small lump on the back of the neck. To parade your knowledge would be as vulgar as to parade your genitals.

Besides, boring other people is a more grievous offence in Britain than it is in the States. Americans are concerned about sin, and the British about bad manners. It is alright in Britain to talk about serious matters as long as you also find a way to make them entertaining. "Amusing" is one of the most affirmative words in the gentleman's vocabulary, and those who display this virtue can generally be forgiven for also being fraudsters or bigamists. As befits a puritan race, Americans tend to make a sharper distinction between what is serious and what is not. There is sometimes more need for a shift of tone to signal that what you are saying is meant to be frivolous, light-hearted or just plain silly.

THREE

Mortal Bodies and Immortal Minds

National Physique

An American student who once walked behind me on a college campus told me later that he knew I was from Britain by the way I walked. Perhaps he found my walk ironic, understated, reserved and self-effacing. I do not believe for a moment that this was a fantasy on his part. There is an American male style of walking, just as there is an English male one. A lot of young American men walk with a slightly hunched, ape-like, shambling gait, legs splayed but one foot turned inwards, as though a horse has just escaped from between their knees without their noticing. They walk as they talk: casual, loose and uncoordinated.

John Malkovich plays an eighteenth-century French noble-man in the movie *Les Liaisons Dangereuses*, but moves like a twentieth-century American. American men are typically big-

ger and rangier than their British counterparts. This means that
at American baseball games we have to be placed on the backs
of burly, beer-swilling spectators so as to see what is going on.
On a U.S. campus I generally feel like Gulliver in Brobdingnag,
expecting one of the colossal youths around me to stoop down,
scoop me up and perch me on his shoulder like a parrot. Everything in the States is on a more epic scale than in Britain,
including its people.

Americans who come to live in Britain or Ireland sometimes
undergo a gradual physical change. When they arrive, not least
if they come from one of the dodgier parts of some large American city, they tend to leap several feet in the air if someone pads
noiselessly up behind them on the sidewalk. After a while, they
begin to relax, unravel their physical reflexes, reconstitute their
nervous system, and take on a different kind of body. They cease
to be horrified by the sight of sugar bowls on café tables, where
the sugar lies open to all kinds of unspeakable infections. An
adventurous few might even come to enjoy the delicacy known
as black pudding, especially if you do not tell them beforehand
that it consists of congealed pig's blood. Some of them can be
brought to confess that bathrooms are not really bathrooms at
all, and that one does not stroll into a restroom to find people
stacked in bunks sound asleep. They might even cease to shriek
hysterically at the smell of cigarette smoke, though this usually
takes a decade or so of intensive de-purification. There have
been suggestions that this process could be speeded up by herd-
ing all visiting Americans into contamination camps, where
they would be coated in cow shit and exposed to a range of non-
lethal viruses in order to accustom them to the mind-shattering
notion that germs and dirt are a regular part of everyday life.

Europeans might receive exactly the opposite treatment when they land in New York.

Physical appearance in Britain is deeply conditioned by class. There is a certain kind of tall, stooped, willowy, long-faced, chinless, floppy-haired aristocrat who could not possibly be mistaken for a mechanic even if he were to wear oil-stained overalls and brandish a wrench. Centuries of fine food and selective breeding play their part in producing this physique, though so occasionally does a spot of incest. Hugh Grant could not possibly be from the working-class—not just on account of his accent, but because of his physiognomy. There is a working-class, North-of-England face which is different from a middle-class, South-of-England one. Jeremy Irons could not hail from anywhere north of Oxford, and Albert Finney is unlikely to come from the so-called Home Counties around London. Bob Hoskins looks like a Cockney as well as talking like one. Prince Charles could not be a Texan, though if the Texans wanted to take him in, there are those among us who would have no principled objection.

I was once on an escalator in the London Underground, puzzling yet again over signs reading "Dogs Must Be Carried," and wondering whether I would be arrested for not clutching a spaniel to my chest, when I noticed a middle-aged man on the escalator opposite standing just behind a young soldier in uniform. The middle-aged man was stout and expensively dressed in a camel-hair overcoat, with swept-back grey hair and a rubicund countenance. Having eyed the soldier's back for a few moments, he murmured, "Put your cap on, Private." The soldier turned, glanced at him for no more than half a second, and replied, "Yes, sir." He then took his cap from his pocket and put it on, and the middle-aged man fell into some good-humoured conversation with him about where he was stationed.

It was clear that the two men did not know each other. But it took the private only the blink of an eye to recognise that despite his civilian dress the man behind him was a high-ranking army officer, and it took me only about the same time. It was not just his straight back, air of authority and imperious accent which gave him away. He had the face of a British colonel or major-general, rather as many Oxford and Cambridge academics have the mild, unused, ascetic faces of Oxford and Cambridge academics. He also had the voice of a high-ranking military officer, which in Britain is different from the voice of a banker or a bishop. If I myself had told the soldier to put his cap on, even though I looked fairly middle-class and was reasonably well dressed, his reply would no doubt have consisted of a couple of abrupt monosyllables.

It is sometimes claimed that Catholics and Protestants in Northern Ireland can identify one another visually. This, one would think, is the ultimate stereotyping fantasy. In fact, there is probably something to it. The two main religious groups in the region stem largely from different ethnic backgrounds. Catholics are for the most part of the same ethnic stock as the Irish to the south of them, whereas Protestants are mostly of Scottish provenance. A woman with jet black hair and blue eyes is likely to be a Catholic, while a stocky, sandy-haired man is probably a Protestant. Of course this does not apply across the board. There are sandy-haired Catholics and black-haired, blue-eyed Protestants, just as there are no doubt people who declaim Dante in Butte, Montana, and taxi drivers in Brooklyn who curl up with a volume of Goethe. But it serves as a rough guide to religious denomination. You can also tell the difference between a Protestant and a Catholic in Northern Ireland by noting the way they pronounce the letter *h*. The former says "aitch" while the latter says "haitch."

Postmodernists tend to be uneasy with this kind of talk. It seems to play down culture while playing up nature and biology, a realm of which postmodernism is unduly nervous. Cultural style is allowed a part in physical appearance, but not genetics. Humanists have always had it in for science, and this is simply the latest phase of that long prejudice. The fact is, however, that the human body, pierce, paint and pummel it as one will, is a given. We do not choose our bodies, and cannot trade them in as we can our trombones. For a civilisation like the United States, which places so much value on choice, control and the constructive will, fleshliness is thus something of a scandal. It seems to be at odds with our self-fashioning. America is unhappy with things that are simply given rather than strenuously created. They smack too much of destiny, which is not among its favourite notions. (Providence is another matter.) This is why the nation has sometimes been reluctant to admit that the land was there before its people got to work on it. It is also why reconstructing the body has become such a heavy industry in today's United States.

Many Americans look different from Europeans, and not just because they wear check shirts or bright pink trouser suits. Simply by their physical appearance, Eisenhower and Billy Graham could have been nothing but American. The same is true of Julia Roberts and Andie MacDowell, though not, ironically, of Sarah Palin. Richard Nixon looked intensely American, and so does John McCain, but the same is not true of Jack Nicholson, Hillary Clinton or Harrison Ford. Mitt Romney looks more

American than Mount Rushmore. To some extent, it is possible to distinguish male Democratic politicians from male Republican ones. On the whole, Republicans look more stereotypically American than Democrats, a fact which may stoke the prejudice that the latter are less patriotic than the former. In general, the squarer the chin, the more likely you are to oppose tax increases. A few more square-jawed, fresh-faced, steely-eyed recruits to the ranks of the Democrats might boost their cause immeasurably.

How you look is vitally important in American politics. Experiments show that even young children can pick the winners of political elections on the basis of photographs alone. Who cares if you believe in nuking Iran as long as your teeth sparkle? A recent Irish prime minister who bore a distinct resemblance to a toad would not have made it to Capitol Hill even as an intern.

There is an ideal of feminine beauty in the States which is distinctly non-European. It favours high cheekbones, thin faces and very wide mouths. Quite a few famous female movie stars in the States look like this. The faces of American women can seem over-expressive to an outsider's eye, with the flesh too tightly moulded to the feeling. American women are also the only group of human beings in the world who sometimes nod as they speak, and then continue to nod for a second or two after they have fallen silent.

Vile Bodies

Physically speaking, American tourists in the centre of London or Dublin are easily identifiable. For one thing, they are usually the most tastelessly dressed of overseas visitors. Many of the men wear tartan, lumberjack-like shirts, which are so common that one suspects they must be issued to all prospective male tourists by the federal government. Perhaps Washington also makes wearing them compulsory, since it is hard to see why else anyone would do so. The old men wear their trousers too high and have bleached, scaly, lizard-like skin, of a kind only ever seen on elderly American males. Shuffling along in twos and threes, they look like a leper colony on a day out.

Tourists from the States also stand out because a good many of them tend to hobble and waddle, being overweight and unused to walking. In fact, by the end of a day in Stratford or Edinburgh, they may well have done more hobbling and waddling than they have done back home for the past ten years. Like other tourists, Americans arrive equipped with a cunning device which saves them from having to look at what they are standing in front of. This is known as a camera or cell phone. Perhaps tourists from different parts of the globe could simply send their cameras and cell phones by mail to various overseas tourist boards, who would take snapshots on their behalf for a modest fee and send them back. This would save prospective visitors a good deal of time, money and painful hobbling.

One of the many paradoxes of the United States is that it is both fleshly and ascetic, worldly and otherworldly. The nation is as metaphysical as it is materialistic. The will which drives you to accumulate goods also detaches you from them. It does so because all such goods are finite, and therefore imperfect. If the will gorges itself upon them, it does so with its gaze fixed steadfastly on infinity. There is something profoundly religious about consumer capitalism, which is one reason why the United States is among the most godly places on earth, as well as one of the most profane.

The balance between engagement and detachment, however, is a hard one to strike. In the States, it tends to tip on the one side towards total immersion, as people triumphantly consume seventy-eight hot dogs in two minutes flat, and on the other side towards a withdrawal from the flesh altogether. In a familiar narcissism, the body becomes an object you carry around with you like some priceless, sickeningly fragile vase. What to put inside it becomes as fraught an issue as what to put in your will. Many of the well-off eat sparingly, which is the only bond they have with the poor. You care for your body not because you love it, but as you might attend to some temperamental beast which is capable of turning on you and savaging you at any moment. There are those who react to being offered an aspirin as though they are being handed a tarantula.

Eating and drinking are acts of transgression, as the purity of one's inner space risks being polluted by a messy material world. The body acts as the symbolic threshold between the two. Poised ambiguously between the two realms, it is fully at home in neither. The body is an ambiguous zone in any case. If it is what binds us to others, it is also what walls us off from them. You can let it run to seed, secure in the knowledge that the real you is buried deep within it ("What matters is what's inside you"). Or you can punish and purify it by running thirty miles a day, converting it into a steel-hard instrument of your will. Either way, the true self is disembodied. It has no truck with the degenerate flesh. The real you is either so deep within the body as to be no part of it, or it manipulates it from a lofty distance.

On Purity and Poison

At worst, a fear of transgression can result in the misery and occasional tragedy of eating disorders, though there are many other ways of accounting for such ailments. It is not, of course, that all those afflicted by such disorders are possessed by the manic will. It is rather that, as Freud knew, there is a psychopathology of everyday life, in which the behaviour of those who are ill and unhappy serves to write large the malaise of a whole civilisation. Western civilisation as a whole has a pathological relation to the material world, of which food and the body are palpable signs. The metaphor of invasion is to be found everywhere in America, from eating to Al Qaeda. An American physician I know was taught in medical school that the way to make real money was to "invade the body." What the British know as burglary is sometimes called home invasion in the United States.

That Americans are overweight is a stale cliché, but it is perhaps less hackneyed to note that one reason for this is their parochialism. Many of them have no idea that the planet is not populated by people just like themselves. Nor could some of them fit into the aircraft seats that might allow them to find out. Admittedly, it is not as though they would instantly shed a hundred pounds if they were to discover that everyone in Armenia or Montenegro is as skinny as Victoria Beckham. Even so, the fact that the United States constitutes a whole universe of its own may make people less troubled by the fact that they need a small crane to swing them out of bed. America is its own norm. It finds it hard to view itself from the outside. It is not greatly taken with cultural comparisons. Euphemism plays a part here too. Obese women are "full figured," fat children are winsomely "chubby," and men who need a whole train compartment to themselves are admired for their "hearty appetite." Beer bellies can be a sign of virility.

Grossly overweight Americans plod cheerfully around unaware that there are some countries in which they would probably be forced to hide in caves, emerging only at dusk to scavenge great mounds of food and drag it furtively back to their hideouts. In some authoritarian regimes, they might even be flushed off the streets along with beggars and prostitutes when some international sporting event hits town. There is, to be sure, a lot of obesity elsewhere on the planet, but nobody is as mind-warpingly, transcendentally enormous as an enormous American. People who are wide enough to block the aisle of a supermarket can be found in the United States, but are far rarer in Europe, though the numbers are growing, thanks to America's multinational purveyors of junk food. It is doubtful that many of them are even to be found hiding in caves in the Pyrenees, assuming they could squeeze into them in the first place.

Perhaps Americans can afford to be obese because they have so much space to expand into. People in the States will say "Excuse me" if they come within ten feet of you, since they are accustomed to having so much of the stuff at their disposal that they expect you to feel intruded on. On the Tokyo subway, by contrast, you can sit in someone's lap for half an hour without their realising. (On the London Underground they would notice but pretend that you weren't there, fearful of making a fuss.) It is an attempt to avoid such trespasses that causes me to write so many books. Reading books by other people has always struck me as an unwarranted invasion of their personal space. This is why when I wish to read a book, I write one. It is a way of respecting the privacy of others.

An English friend of mine who visited the United States for the first time came back with only one scene recorded on his videocamera. It was of a freight train, passing silently and endlessly, apparently without end or origin, with ridiculously more cars than one would see in Europe. It was an image of infinity. Like God, America seems to go on forever. Bits and pieces of it are scattered throughout the globe. It crops up wherever you look, like heartache or cherry blossom. Perhaps there is a secret U.S. colony on Saturn. The nation compensates for the brevity of its history with the boundlessness of its space. The American self is more likely than the European soul to see itself as infinite, partly because it has so little history to hamper it, and partly because it has so much space to spread into. If Europe is smothered beneath history, America languishes for lack of it.

Bumming a Fag

When it comes to the body, there is also the question of smoking. One of the several American objections to the habit, one that encapsulates many of the nation's phobias and anxieties, is that it constitutes a kind of illicit connection between people, shrinking the space to which they can rightfully lay claim. It is a symbolic mingling of bodies, and as such offensive to American individualism. Another objection is that smoking is a pure act of ingestion, one which, unlike eating, lacks all biological value or necessity. As such, it symbolises the transgressive movement, from outer to inner and out again, in its starkest form.

It is true that the American aversion to smoking is at root eminently rational, given the horrendous consequences of the habit. But the moral fervour with which the subject has been invested in the States, along with the zeal with which the hapless smoker is sometimes hounded, suggests that there is more to the matter than rationality. It is possible to act unreasonably in a reasonable cause. Smoking in the States is never just smoking, rather as one sometimes suspects that the last thing food is is food. Smoking represents a sinister infiltration of the other into one's hygienically sealed world. America thus has its fair share of smoking fascists. There have been literal smoking fascists too. Hitler was fanatically opposed to the habit, and banned it from his bunker even as Soviet tanks were bearing down on it. He was also hysterical about germs, a neurosis shared by many middle-class Americans. There is some evidence that Osama bin Laden also banished smoking from his compound, though it is unlikely that his image will be blazoned on U.S. anti-smoking posters.

In America as in Europe, the anti-smoking campaign is basically a class conspiracy. By and large, the working class continue to smoke while the middle class have given it up. Banning cigarettes is clearly an attempt to entrench middle-class power over a working class whose demise may now be literal as well as sociological. Many middle-class Americans seem to have abandoned drinking as well. I once came across a couple of American acquaintances of mine sitting at a table in the bar of a Dublin theatre without even an orange juice in front of them. You can be prosecuted for that in Ireland. In today's China, by contrast, heavy drinking can get you promoted, while moderate imbibing can ruin your professional prospects. One can harm one's career by not downing an excessive number of drinks with one's colleagues. Job advertisements sometimes explicitly ask for applicants who can hold their drink. "Candidates with good drinking capacity will be given priority," read one for an engineering company. It is hard to imagine a similar ad for Goldman Sachs. If you are a binge drinker, which is true of over half the men and more than a quarter of the women who drink in China, it may be advisable to mention it on your CV. There is certainly no other way in which it is likely to smooth your progress through life.

Middle-class America is rather more abstemious. Charles Dickens complains in his *American Notes* about the absence of alcohol in his hotel, where he is forced to drink tea and coffee instead. "This preposterous forcing of unpleasant drinks down the reluctant throats of travellers," he grumbles, "is not at all uncommon in America." Perhaps it was not uncommon then, but it was certainly untrue of the early American Puritans. Drinking alcohol was quite acceptable to them, if only because their water tended to be contaminated by human and animal waste, milk before pasteurisation was risky, and coffee, tea and chocolate were yet to catch on. It is true that the Irish do not require such austerely rational grounds for knocking back booze, or indeed any rational grounds at all, but neither did the early Puritans. There was regular feasting and partying among them, along with singing and even card-playing. One Puritan minister wrote that sexual intercourse should be conducted "willingly, often, and cheerfully." He meant, of course, between husband and wife. The earliest American immigrants enjoyed themselves a lot more than some of their grim-faced progeny. They also differed from them in their profound respect for tradition, as well as in their vision of human society as an organic whole.

It was a lack of fun that struck Dickens about America, long before the fun industry was invented there. He found its earnestness mildly oppressive. Philadelphia seemed to him "distractingly regular. After walking about it for an hour or two, I felt that I would have given the world for a crooked street. The collar of my coat appeared to stiffen, and the brim of my hat to expand, beneath its Quakerly influence. My hair shrunk into a sleek short crop, my hands folded themselves upon my breast of their own calm accord, and thoughts of . . . making a large fortune by speculations in corn, came over me involuntarily." Speaking of Calvinist gloom, he confesses that "I so abhor, and from my soul detest that bad spirit, no matter by what class or sect it may be entertained, which would strip life of its healthful graces, rob youth of its innocent pleasures, pluck from maturity and age their pleasant ornaments, and make existence but a narrow path towards the grave." There is an odious spirit of "stiff-necked solemn-visaged piety" abroad in the nation, which a writer who at one level clearly prefers his Fagin to his Oliver Twist finds hard to stomach. He would have been astounded by Las Vegas. Since Dickens's day, pleasure and enjoyment have been among the United States's most precious heritage to humanity.

Tidying the body away to avoid unpleasantness is a familiar American practice. People do not die, they pass away, rather as an exploding spaceship is not a calamity but an anomaly. Toilets or lavatories become restrooms or bathrooms. The British find it amusing to be asked by American tourists on trains where the bathroom is. Being a disgustingly unhygienic bunch, they would never dream of taking a bath on a train themselves. I once overheard a young American tourist phoning home to her mother in the middle of Dublin. "Mom," she whispered, aghast, "they have stores here full of dead animals!" She presumably meant butcher's shops. These days in the States, the Mafia probably wrap their victims in Saran Wrap before hoisting them on to meat hooks.

Samuel Butler's novel *Erewhon*, published in late-nineteenth-century England, portrays a civilisation in which illness is seen as a moral defect, while vice is regarded as a kind of disease. The latter view is untypical of America, since it smacks too much of moral determinism. Nor do Americans see illness as a moral failing. Some of them, however, seem to feel that it is morally offensive to take a negative view of it. Developing cancer may not be anti-American, but complaining about it certainly can be. Barbara Ehrenreich notes in her invaluable *Smile or Die* that breast cancer is often referred to in the United States as a "gift." Some sufferers wouldn't be without it, just as they wouldn't be without their Siamese cats or Shetland sweaters. Instead of being life-changing in the sense of killing you, it is life-changing in the sense of making you a more caring, sensitive person. There are those of us who would prefer to be brutal, insensitive and alive.

Given the American penchant for euphemism, it is a wonder that dying is not spoken of as "transformatively transitioning," as in "Seven of the rebels were wounded, and three others were transformatively transitioned." In the same upbeat vein, being thrown out of work is sometimes redefined by the magic of the signifier as a "career-changing opportunity." Only whiners would object that some changes are undesirable. Some Americans seem to hold the bizarre view that change is a good in itself, as though swapping your brandy and soda for a cup of cold vomit is bound to represent an imaginative leap forward. They would be astounded by Samuel Johnson's remark that all change is a great evil. They would also be right to reject it, though not because all change is a great good.

The Pleasures of Indolence

It is no secret that Americans are deeply anxious about their bodies. In fact, if U.S. television ads are to be believed, they are worried about them to the point of mass psychosis. A nation's media is not of course a faithful image of its actual life. If that were the case, all Americans would be in a permanent state of orgasmic joy, would never cease to grin manically or have toddlers tumble joyously all over them, and would have teeth so sparkling that those around them would need shades. When I once visited an American dentist plagued by acute toothache, I was surprised to find that the first question on the form I had to fill out was "What do you feel about your smile?" This seemed rather like being asked how you felt about your hairstyle when admitted to hospital for brain surgery.

The media, needless to say, do not habitually tell it like it is. Even so, they distil something of a culture's abiding preoccupations, in however monstrously distorted a guise. In this sense they are rather like dreams, which present real thoughts and desires in garbled, disfigured form. If the social unconscious of the United States is to be credited, all is not well with the flesh and blood of the Land of the Free. Americans today have a problem about being incarnate creatures, rather as their Puritan forefathers did. They would not readily agree with Thomas Aquinas that human rationality is an animal rationality, and that it is the body, not some disembodied mind or spirit, that is the criterion of human identity. Aquinas would have believed in the existence of the disembodied soul of Jimi Hendrix, but he would not have believed that it was Jimi Hendrix. American culture is typically more dualistic, as befits a people so extraordinarily idealistic that the mind can never feel quite at home with anything as lowly as matter.

Take, for example, the business of staying in bed. Among the hard-working American middle classes, this is not the most popular of pastimes. Americans tend to rise in the morning earlier than Europeans, and go to bed earlier as well. There are clear economic motives for this, but also, one suspects, a queasy puritan sense that indulging the body by not dragging it brutally out of bed at the crack of dawn is somewhat sinful. An American mother I know used to run the washing machine and make school lunches for her children at three o'clock in the morning. People who do this should be handed lengthy prison sentences. Visitors to the States who stay in hotels will have had the traumatic experience of hearing what sounds like a dam bursting around six o'clock in the morning. This is the sound of fifty showers being switched on, at an hour when any civilised human being would still be agreeably unconscious.

Americans do not seem to realise what a rich, fruitful, endlessly fascinating pursuit staying in bed can be. Rather as English aristocrats have taken centuries to perfect the art of doing nothing at all, a strenuous, demanding affair which requires a good deal of skill, persistence and unflinching concentration, so staying in bed can be a passion, a vocation, a religion, an existential commitment, a whole way of life. Those who stay in bed form a kind of secret spiritual aristocracy. They are a cosmopolitan confraternity, recognisable to each other by certain shyly murmured passwords and esoteric handshakes. Sometimes they compete with each other to see who can remain supine until dinner time, sternly suppressing any ignoble impulse to get up. They do not regard sleeplessness as a virtue, any more than insomniacs do.

Americans, by contrast, like to be up and doing. They find it hard to savour the delights of passivity. They are relatively unfamiliar with the spiritual treasures to be reaped from being acted on rather than acting. For them, there is something both guilt-making and unmanly about such a condition. Steve Jobs's sister, thinking she was paying him a compliment, described his death as something he "achieved." Simply to have something happen to you is unthinkable. It undermines the vital business of being in control. Bed is where the body refreshes itself in order to plunge back into action. To enjoy it for its own sake is mildly perverse, rather like enjoying having rabies. The Duke of Edinburgh was once horrified to discover that his son Prince Charles actually reads in bed. Reading for the Duke is something of a degenerate activity in any case, but to confuse sleeping and waking life in this way struck him as morally pernicious. Bed is a preparation for activity, not a condition to be enjoyed in itself. It is certainly not a place in which to indulge such wimpish pursuits as learning about the secrets of the Pyramids or the inner life of vegetables, as the New Ageist Charles probably does.

Nature and the Will

America's disquiet with the body is not just the familiar tale of dieting, obesity, frenetic exercising, or trying to thread your jaws together with wire and a pair of pliers in front of the bathroom mirror. The country has a problem with the body because it has a problem with the finite. The desire which drives the nation— its hunger for progress, achievement, expansion, advancement, possession, consumption—is an infinite one which brooks no restraint. On this view, there are no natural limits to aspiration, only those obstacles thrown up by one's failure to achieve. It is a vision of reality far removed from Macbeth's "I dare do all that may become a man;/Who dares do more is none." It does not see that some confines are creative rather than obstructive, some limits enabling rather than impeding. In a time-worn Romantic fallacy, expansion and self-expression are viewed as good in themselves, and what is bad is whatever reins them in. One thing which thwarts them is the body, which must therefore be worked upon intensively. Human flesh is appallingly feeble. It must be disciplined and remoulded if anything good is to be plucked from it, rather as some conservatives hold that people must be bawled out and knocked around if they are to give of their best.

On this view, what is supremely positive is the will. In a certain sense, it is all that exists. The will is a raw force that pounds the world into order, and occasionally pounds it to pieces. This includes the body, which is the bit of the material world which is part of us. In order to shape things to its needs, however, the will risks knocking the stuffing out of them, leaving them void, valueless, and so not really worth shaping in the first place. Yet it can do its work all the better if there is no meaning inherent in the world itself. Once things are drained of significance, they put up less resistance to one's projects. Reality becomes endlessly pliable stuff. It can be pummelled into whatever form you fancy, as in the gym or cosmetic surgery. "Political principles, laws, and human institutions," comments de Tocqueville of America, "seem malleable things which can at will be adopted and combined." Maybe even our mortality will buckle in the end to the all-conquering mind. Among the most typically American features of Michael Jackson was the fact that he wanted to live forever, a wish which not every member of the world's population was eager to see realised.

The will lies at the core of the self, which means that the self is what bestows meaning and value on things. But the self is also part of material reality. So we, too, are part of what has to be hammered into shape. We are clay in our own hands, awaiting the moment when we will transform ourselves into an artefact of great splendour. The self is always a work in progress. It is a kind of wilderness which must be cultivated, mixed with one's labour, before it can become meaningful. It is part of Puritan doctrine that human labour is what makes things real. Before we happened along, there was just chaos. Ceaseless activity is what keeps the world in existence. American optimism thus conceals a darker vision. It springs as much from a scepticism about material reality as from an affirmation of it. In themselves, Nature and the flesh are chaotic stuff. They are worthless until the spirit invests them with significance. It is labour that transforms Nature into meaning. And this always involves a degree of violence. Body and soul are both subject to belligerent onslaughts, along with rain forests and terrorist strongholds.

A lot of the West's running, carving, slimming, stitching, puking and weight-pumping represents a fantasy of omnipotence, but also of immortality. It betrays a deep-seated hostility to the body, over which the immortal will must assert its sway. Because it is fragile, the body must be nurtured tenderly, yet it is just this fragility that makes you feel so squeamish about it. In the end, however, Nature always has the upper hand over culture. This victory is known as death. Death cannot be mastered, and is thus bound to be something of an indignity for those who wish the world to be magically responsive to their touch. There is nothing you can do with it. A corpse is just a lump of meaningless matter. Its meaning has haemorrhaged away.

Tragedy is the wager that you can make something out of this dissolution, plucking value from loss and breakdown. You can do so, however, only by staring these things squarely in the face. Only by submitting to their power can you transcend them. It is this that America finds hard to accept. In this as in other ways, it is a profoundly anti-tragic civilisation. On the whole, it rejects the belief, common to both St. Paul and Martin Heidegger, that you can make something of your life only by making something of your death.

Before the pioneers set out on their civilising mission, there was, so they imagined, simply wilderness. This wilderness was not entirely real, because it was yet to have meaning stamped upon it by the human will. Even so, America has always been nostalgic for this condition. In a world in which everything bears the indelible impress of Man, it is refreshing to escape from time to time from this wall-to-wall humanisation. Hence the American enthusiasm for national parks and outdoor activities. It is seductive to see the world as though we were not there to see it. We can always dream of perceiving things as they are in themselves, without the buzz and distortion of human meaning. We can take a vacation now and then from the intolerable burden of sense-making, rather as we do when we treat human flesh as something to be mindlessly indulged. We can shuck off language and confront reality in the raw, as we imagine an innocent child might do.

Man is what brings Nature to perfection, but he is also an intruder there. There is a strong streak of such primitivism in American culture. It is all the stronger because the wilderness was not that long ago, and because it still flourishes in the sublime rivers and mountain ranges of the country. It is worth adding, however, that though Nature in the United States is more dramatic and spectacular than most of the British countryside, it is not what one would call charming, as Cornish villages and the Yorkshire Dales are charming. Charm is more of a European quality than an American one. It is hard to be charming on a large scale, not least in a country where individual states dwarf entire European countries.

Yet there was also something ominous about this untamed landscape. It could be a place for spiritual reflection, or a refuge from a wicked world; but it was also an image of the brutish, anarchic self, which the early Puritans feared and sought to subdue. The wilderness could be seen as a barren waste land or spiritual darkness where the Devil lurked. Only through the sweated labour of men and women could anything decent and godly be made of it. Meaning and truth issue from the hand of Man. To make something intelligible is to draw it from the demon-ridden darkness into the sacred clearing illuminated by the light of reason. In subjugating the world in obedience to the word of Genesis, Man himself becomes a mini-Creator, conjuring order out of chaos. The belief that truth is a human creation, a popular doctrine in

American philosophy, harks back to this vision. Without Man, the world withers.

Alexis de Tocqueville, who thought, incidentally, that America had less interest in philosophy than any other civilised nation, writes in proto-Marxist style of the conquest of Nature in early America. "The American people," he remarks, "see themselves as marching through wildernesses, drying up marshes, diverting rivers, peopling the wilds, and subduing nature." Yet the land, he argues, was not fertile enough to sustain a prosperous class of landlords alongside one of tenants, so there was no material basis in the country for an aristocracy. For that, you need large estates, not parcelled-out pieces of soil. He also points out that America's encounter with the wilderness threw European history into reverse. Whereas Europeans evolved from so-called barbarism to civilisation, the early immigrants to America confronted a supposedly virgin Nature while themselves being "the product of eighteen centuries of labour and experience."

As an immense region of untapped natural resources, America lay at the feet not of noble savages who would have been incapable of utilising it, but of educated, urban-bred, sophisticated men who plunged into its forests furnished with "Bible, axe, and newspapers." The country, in short, was born of a felicitous time warp. For the newcomers, if not for the natives, it was the most fortunate conjuncture imaginable between the wild and the cultivated. What greater capitalist fantasy than that of an industrious people suddenly supplied with limitless natural resources to be exploited? It is the Robinson Crusoe myth on a spectacular scale. No wonder the nation was thought to be a work of Providence.

Anything Is Possible

Because of the all-powerful will, Americans are great believers in the fraudulent doctrine that you can do anything you want if you try hard enough. In no other country on earth does one hear this consoling lie chanted so often. If you want to fly to Rio and there is no airport to hand, simply want it as hard as you can and feathers will sprout spontaneously from your biceps. When the United States finally killed Osama bin Laden, Barack Obama declared with mathematical predictability that it was an example of how the country could do anything it set its mind to. He did not mention that ten years is a rather long time for the omnipotent will to creak into action. One wonders why the nation does not put its mind to abolishing poverty, if all of its mental strivings are guaranteed to succeed. The United States has a larger proportion of its population in prison, higher levels of mental illness, greater rates of teenage pregnancy, a lower level of child well-being, and higher levels of poverty and social exclusion than most other developed nations. Perhaps this is because its people have not been exercising their wills in concert. Perhaps a date and time should be appointed for, say, the willing away of criminal gangs, when great hordes of people can emerge civic-mindedly on to the streets and bend their collective mental efforts to this end.

The will is a modern substitute for the Almighty. Men and women can achieve great things by its power, but since to the puritan mind they are naturally given to devilish devices, this will come about only if they are constantly prodded, spurred on, mentored, exhorted, preached at and morally browbeaten. Otherwise they will lapse back into their natural-born turpitude.

Hence the constant moralising, sermonising and cheer-leading of American society. It is no wonder that it venerates sports coaches as much as it does, given that they spend their time bawling at people to improve their performance.

It was a communal act of willing that brought America about in the first place. The nation itself is the work of the will. It is not just a country like any other, but a project, a vocation, a mission, a destiny, a spiritual enterprise. Nobody thinks this about Belgium. It is not the case with Wales, Slovenia or the United Arab Emirates, which some Americans might suspect is a movie company. Britain is not the work of the will. The British never planned their empire, for example. It just fell into their lap in a fit of absent-mindedness. They awoke one morning to find that they were governing India, even though nothing had been further from their thoughts. They did not particularly savour the prospect, but it seemed churlish not to get on with it.

Other countries just grew, while America was deliberately thought up. It is more like an automobile than an amoeba. It is unlike other nations not just because it is richer and has more jet fighters, but because it is less a chunk of land than a Platonic ideal. The United States has been called by God to be a model for other nations, which is to say that it is the very essence and paradigm of what nationhood is meant to be. It is not just a nation but *the* nation, rather as a Hoover is the very archetype of a vacuum cleaner. There are places in the world where patriotism has replaced religion, not least in the case of nationalist movements. In America, patriotism is a form of religion in itself, since it reveres one of God's most precious creations, the nation.

Whether the country is strong and prosperous because it has been divinely chosen, or whether it was chosen because it was strong and prosperous, is not entirely clear. It was not because of their individual merit that the Jews were Yahweh's favoured people. They were simply born into this chosen nation. The same is true of Americans. You do not normally choose to be an American, any more than you choose to be covered in freckles. It is not in that sense a matter of innate qualities. Yet it is hard to avoid the feeling that God chose the United States as his number one nation because he recognised its inherent merit, foreseeing that in the fullness of time its gross national product would be so impressive. Perhaps he is already turning his attention to China, India and Brazil, countries which as far as affluence goes seem to be rising rapidly in the most-favoured-people-under-God stakes. The Almighty may be a more fickle being than Americans suspect. It may be that the United States's favoured-nation contract is running out, and that the Creator will be reluctant to renew it. It is also not clear whether countries need to have nuclear weapons to be acceptable in his sight, though it probably does no harm.

The Perils of Idealism

Ideals are what the will aims at, and the United States is an idealist nation in a double sense of the word. It is strongly committed to certain lofty goals, and it is idealist in the philosophical sense of believing that the mind creates reality. There is a connection between the two, since if you pitch your ideals as high as America does, you will need nothing short of an all-powerful mind to achieve them. The former kind of idealism is commendable but also cruel. Men and women need goals to aim at; but if these ideals are unrealistic, all they will do is rub their noses in their failure to attain them. The result will be self-hatred and abysmally low self-esteem. There is something terroristic about such idealism, as there is something terroristic for Freud about the superego. For Freud, the superego is not only vindictive but obtuse. It punishes us with obscene delight for falling short of ideals it should know we cannot achieve.

The enemy of the superego is comedy, which accepts our frailty and deficiency with a wry shrug. It converts feeling bad about ourselves into laughing at ourselves, which is not the most popular of American pursuits. We are indeed defective, but this is in the nature of things. It is also bound up with what is precious about us. The spirit of comedy is the spirit of forgiveness. Impurity is to be relished as well as put right, whereas the puritan mind refuses to accept anything less than perfection. This is one reason why it is so allergic to the material, a messy phenomenon which can never be wholly mastered by an idea. It will always come seeping out over the edges of our schemes, like some ghastly piece of ectoplasm.

It is tragedy, not comedy, which holds that the truth about men and women stands revealed only when you purge them of their everyday habits and press them to an extreme. This, too, is a typically American article of faith, though without the tragic implications. Real human beings are those who push themselves to a limit. You will know who you really are only when you are up against the wall. Life is a race, a trial, a competition, a set of hurdles, and to succeed in it you must be constantly on your toes, in moral training, perpetually at your best. To march on the spot is to fall behind.

That the superego is so implacable is why St. Paul thinks that the Law is cursed. It can only show us where we go wrong, not inspire us to do right. Those who languish in the grip of excessive idealism risk falling ill of it. They are the slaves of a particularly brutal master. Human beings, Freud remarked, are both more and less moral than they think they are. If they are too neurotic about morality, they will be less moral in a more important sense of the term, less able to live a richly self-fulfilling existence. If the United States could be a little less moral, it would be greatly to its advantage. In fact, the nation might become more moral by being less so. It is partly because the country is so much in the grip of certain high-minded doctrines that it sometimes behaves so shabbily. It is ready to sacrifice the lives of small children in foreign lands to its own spiritual certainties.

What is negative, then, is whatever stands in the way of the will. And this, as we have seen, includes the amorphous matter that the will seeks to reduce to order. This is why one of the most materialistic civilisations on earth harbours a secret hostility to the material. Mary Baker Eddy, founder of that quintessentially American creed, Christian Science, thought the material world was an illusion. Many Americans are in this sense natural-born Buddhists. Yet the doctrine of mind over matter, which accounts for so much in American culture, is strangely self-refuting. It sees the mind as independent of material circumstance, but fails to recognise that this belief is itself shaped by material conditions. From the Pilgrim Fathers to Pepsi-Cola, America has had good material reasons for moulding the earth to its desires. It is not, of course, the only nation to have done so. Mastering Nature is a necessity for any civilisation, whatever the more dewy-eyed kind of eco-warrior might think. Unless we build some sea walls pretty quickly, Bangladesh may be lost without a trace in some years' time, along with a lot of other places. Diabetics who inject themselves with insulin are seeking to overpower a Nature that has spun out of control. So are engineers who lord it arrogantly over the natural world by building bridges to stop people from drowning. When it comes to blowing up meteors about to strike the earth, a spot of civilised violence does nobody any harm.

Yet violence is not always in the cause of civility. Freud acknowledged that Eros, builder of cities, involves a good deal of aggression. But he also thought that this violence could easily get out of hand. Lurking inside the drive to create and construct was his old enemy Thanatos, or the death drive. The very forces that make for civilisation can also reduce it to chaos and barbarism. Freud would thus have had no problem in understanding what happened not long ago in Iraq, as well as in many other spots where the American eagle has landed and unsheathed its claws. To save the world, you may have to destroy it.

Weak Flesh and Willing Spirits

The world-crushing will is part of America's Puritan legacy. Yet if the United States is such a puritanical nation, how come there are so many strip joints around? What is one to make of a county in which clubs and bars stay open all night while people go to bed at 9 p.m.? This is not as contradictory as it appears. For one thing, revelling in the flesh is simply the flipside of the disembodied will. Those who are hostile to the body can see it only as a source of mindless sensation. Pole dancers and prostitutes are bodies stripped of meaning and value, reduced to brute materiality. People who pour booze into themselves all night long see their flesh simply as a convenient container. This is logical enough if one regards material things not as meaningful in themselves, but as imbued with meaning only by the human will.

For another thing, bare flesh is big business, and to the puritan mind making profit can be a sign of God's favour. It may be that when the Creator urged us to make use of our worldly talents, he did not exactly have pole dancing in mind. Even so, prospering on earth may be a foretaste of flourishing in heaven. This, as it happens, is not the case for the New Testament, which tells us in traditional Judaic spirit that we shall know God for who he is when we see the poor being filled with good things and the rich being sent empty away. The only problem is that those who seek to act on this information might end up with a bullet through the head. This is not a problem over which Mormons and right-wing Evangelicals in the States lose an excessive amount of sleep.

The idea that the flesh is just meaningless matter is a peculiarly modern one. For an older style of thought, the human body is inherently meaningful. In fact, human meaning is in the first place carnal meaning. To watch a small child reaching for a toy even before it can speak is to see this in action. The meaning is inherent in the physical gesture, like the lining in a glove. On this view, the world, which includes our bodies, is significantly organised. It is true that this built-in significance will come to fruition only when we give it voice. The creative human word is an essential part of how things become themselves. But it is not just an arbitrary imposition on them. It must respect the inherent natures of things. It cannot just make what it likes of them, rather as humanity cannot make what it likes of itself.

Among other things, this is because we do not own our-selves, as some modern thinkers seem to imagine. I can use my Victorian paperweight as a door-stopper, but I cannot make what I like of my passions and desires. My body is not my prop-erty. There may be some good arguments for abortion, but the belief that the body is one's private possession is not one of them. For one thing, I can give my property away, but I cannot give my body away. I do not have a pain in the same sense that I have a chain saw. I am not monarch of my own flesh. On the contrary, it is my body, derived as it is from the bodies of others, which proclaims how dependent I am on creatures of my kind. To try to shuck off the body—to regard it as no part of one's real self—is to deny this dependence in the name of an ethic of self-ownership.

If the body is offensive to this ethic, it is because it repre-sents the "outside" of oneself that one can never fully master. At some point in the future, it is going to give up on me whether I like it or not. In this sense, the cosmetic surgeons are playing a losing game. The American dream of immortality sounds like the fantasy of those so deeply in love with life that they cannot bear to relinquish it. In fact, it reflects a virulent hostility to human existence, which is always perishable, incarnate exis-tence. Those who have their sights fixed on earthly immortality are unable to live in the present, and so, ironically, have less to lose from dying than those who can live in the here and now.

American society, as opposed to individual Americans, behaves as though it will never die, and to this extent lives in bad faith. Death is a true satirist, a great deflater and debunker. It cuts us down to our true size. Perhaps all bankers, generals, politicians and corporate executives should be required to undergo near-death experiences in controlled laboratory conditions. It would transform their lives far more thoroughly than any number of courses in packaged Kabala, cut-price Sufism, off-the-peg mysticism, or ready-to-serve transcendentalism. In the case of the more unsavoury bankers and politicians, one might arrange for the experiment to be a little less controlled than it might otherwise be.

The will was not always thought of as a dominative force. For some thinkers in pre-modern times, it is a kind of spontaneous attraction to what is good. It is really a kind of love. For Thomas Aquinas, it means that our bodies have a built-in bias towards the good, which suggests that we are not free to choose whatever ends we like. It is as though some of our ends are chosen for us already, simply by virtue of the kind of creatures we are. We are naturally inclined to happiness and well-being. Far from being a despotic power, the will on this view is a question of one's deepest desires, which are always at root a desire for the good. We can, of course, be spectacularly wrong about what the good consists in, but we cannot not will it.

Since we do not always know what the good consists in, or what our real desires are, the will is not just a question of conscious decision. It cannot be reduced to the callow postmodern cult of "options." To speak of the will of God is not to suggest that the Almighty has a dazzling range of possibilities at his disposal, like a shopper faced with a bewildering array of exotic fruits. God cannot will whatever he pleases. He cannot will evil or sickness. If the will is bound up with our deepest wants and needs, it is not as free as the modern age imagines, any more than our desires are entirely free. One does not choose to desire forgiveness or a grand piano. For Aquinas, a truly free will is not one that can will whatever takes its fancy. It is one that is free from the perversity that drives us to desire what is destructive. The will is not to be seen as boundless and disembodied. It is as finite as a coffee spoon and as fallible as the pope.

There is a sense in which American materialism is a highly spiritual affair. Because the will to possess aspires to infinity, it has all the disdain for material things of a monk or a hippie. It hankers after tangible goods, while being in itself unworldly and austere. This is one reason why it can be reconciled so easily with religion. It is not just hypocrisy for a chief executive to fire two thousand employees and then read a lesson in church on the blessedness of the poor. As a form of infinity, the will that drives the system is on terms with the Almighty. It is an image of him on earth. It is just as bodiless as he is. God transcends the universe as a whole, while the drive to acquire transcends any specific bit of it. The closest thing to not needing anything, which is the enviable condition of God, is not needing something but needing everything.

Desire does not rest easy with the present and particular, since there is an endless future to be won. Capitalism has worked wonders, as Karl Marx never ceased to insist, but there is one achievement that must forever elude it: the ability, as D. H. Lawrence put it, "to live on the spot where we are." Will or desire is radically homeless. The manic will of Captain Ahab in *Moby-Dick* is an utterly unearthly force. Like all infinite things, it is terrifying and annihilating. It can come to rest only in the unattainable Otherness which the white whale signifies. And to do so it will clamber over the whole of Creation.

FOUR

America the Dutiful

A Very Fine American

Unlike Americans, the British are a notoriously godless bunch. They treat their religion rather like alcohol. It is when religious faith starts to interfere with one's everyday life that it is time to give it up. The odd weekly drinking session, like the weekly visit to church, does nobody any harm, but bingeing on the Almighty is as bad for your health as getting smashed on vodka. God is a splendid chap, but there is no point in letting him go to your head. Brood on him too long and before you know where you are you will be breaking down bedroom doors and dragging adulterers out of each other's arms. It is imprudent to take things to extremes. Religious faith may have caused Jesus to be crucified, but that was in another country, and a long time ago. One should find a way of worshipping him which is compatible with support for the monarchy and the odd luxury cruise in the Mediterranean.

Elsewhere in the Western world, sport has largely replaced

religion as a weekly ceremony in which ordinary men and women worship superior beings. In the States, the two forms of liturgy continue to exist side by side. If sport is so vital to American life, it is because it writes large the qualities most valued in everyday existence: strength, heroism, glamour, spectacle, self-discipline, stamina, recklessness, a winning spirit, a consuming desire for wealth, and ferocious competitiveness. It is as though it incarnates the very essence of American life, rather as a man with a beret, an accordion and a string of onions round his neck signifies Frenchness. I was once crossing the campus of a university famous for its football team when I was suddenly assailed by a small posse of security guards, who held me back as though I were an enraged crowd about to storm an embassy. On a signal from one of the guards, a line of football players, each one a precious commodity on legs as thick as tree trunks, plodded slowly from one field to another and disappeared from view. I was then allowed to proceed. Americans are religious about sport, and in this are like many other nations. Most other nations, however, are less religious about religion.

In the United States, Christianity needs to be sanitised, modernised, de-Judaised and Americanised, a project which is known among other things as the Mormon Church. The scandal that Jesus was a scruffy, unhygienic Jew from a part of the globe sorely bereft of bath tubs and chocolate chip cookies must somehow be rectified. So must the fact that he is even more remote from us in time than Gary Cooper. His message must be streamlined and updated, translated into the mission statements of business schools. Such schools usually run courses on business ethics, a subject which a cynical observer might regard as falling into the same category as research into unicorns. In a world of swindling financiers and chief executive gangsters, there is a sense in which Centers for Business Ethics are urgently necessary. One might also argue that they make about as much sense as an Institute for the Advanced Study of Elves.

God is a very fine American because he is such a fantastic success. He knows everything, can do anything, can hire and fire his underlings as the fancy takes him, and despite being omnipotent is admirably upright. This is a rare enough combination on earth, where power and virtue tend to be in inverse proportion to each other. There could be no better role model for an aspiring entrepreneur. God is not dependent on anyone else, and as such is a kind of cosmic advertisement for American individualism. He is unbelievably enormous and powerful and so is the United States, which makes it logical that he should have a special place for the country in his heart.

It is true that the Creator's best-known product, the universe, leaves something to be desired. It is widely acknowledged to be riddled with some alarming flaws and defects, and might well benefit from being taken back to the drawing board. Perhaps the project was overambitious. All the same, you have to hand it to someone who can manufacture such a stupendous product so cheaply, using no materials whatsoever. You can even share in the Lord's success, rather as you can buy shares in Walmart. This is known as grace. The Supreme Being is also remarkable for having cornered the market in universes, at least as far as we know. Certainly no other such product has appeared so far.

Given all this, it is not hard to see why religion and political ideology in the States can be so beautifully blended. Much of the former is simply the latter in thin disguise. It is true that God does not seem to have passed on his success ethic to his immediate family. His son hung out with losers, crooks and whores, and never did a decent day's work in his life. If there had been state handouts in first-century Palestine, he would probably have been first in line to grab them. One can easily picture him as a union agitator, demagogically organising Galilean carpenters. He also probably supported socialised medicine. No doubt it became painfully clear to his distraught parents that he lacked a winning attitude. He refused to settle down, father a number of beautiful, supremely talented children, and contribute to society as an upright citizen. Instead, he denounced the rich, was deserted by his companions, and tortured and murdered by the imperial state. He warned his comrades that if they were true to his word, they, too, would find themselves on death row. Those who did not get themselves executed were simply not trying hard enough. It is true that Jesus is believed to have risen from the dead, which is more than can be said for Michael Jackson, so far at least. But the fact remains that he was scarcely a shining success while he was alive, and according to some Biblical scholars might well have transferred his mission to Jerusalem (a fatal decision, as it turned out) because it was running out of steam in his home territory of Galilee.

One of the most fundamental differences between the United States and Europe is that in the States the twinkly-eyed, grandfatherly type serving you in the local store is quite likely to believe that most of his fellow humans are destined for hellfire, a band of reprobates which almost certainly includes yourself. Yet he will pack your groceries for all the world as though you were not sunk irredeemably in moral squalor, and with touching generosity of spirit show not the slightest hesitation in accepting money from a sinner. It is a striking thought that people who fix exhaust pipes, drink Budweiser and watch ice hockey also believe in demons. It is as though the president of the World Bank were to be caught chalking pentangles on the walls of his office.

There are, needless to say, conflicts as well as affinities between the puritan self and the commercial one. The puritan self mistrusts appearances, whereas the commercial self is all about semblance and self-presentation. When Americans appear on television, they tend to smile when they first come on camera. Nobody does this in Europe. One of the finest of BBC Television's overseas correspondents has not been seen to smile for the last twenty years, and addresses the camera with the expression of one scowling down the barrel of a rifle. To add insult to injury, the journalist in question is a woman. Christopher Hitchens was never known to smile in public. The same goes for his friend, the novelist Martin Amis. Dick Cheney rarely smiles either, but this in a U.S. politician is highly unusual. Perhaps this is because when he does smile, he looks rather like the Wolf about to bite Little Red Riding Hood. Some Irish musicians are so obsessed with self-presentation that they perform with their backs to the audience, a habit which it is hard to imagine Madonna adopting. The United States believes that appearances are all-important, but also that what happens inside you is what really counts. As Walt Whitman almost remarked, if I contradict myself, well, whatever . . .

Prohibition

For many of its adherents, religion is essentially about prohibition. Puritan societies tend to be punitive ones. Bodies and their

appetites can easily get out of hand, and need to be sternly dis-
iplined. This is not the case in Amsterdam, where it is said that
if you sodomise a donkey on the sidewalk, you can receive a state
grant for street theatre. This has never been known to happen
in Grand Rapids. Countries like the United States, which regard
your success as entirely your own doing, also tend to see your
failure as your fault and nobody else's, and to penalise you
accordingly. To point out that you failed at being a world-class
concert pianist because you were born with no arms is a con-
temptible cop-out. It is a refusal to accept responsibility for your
own actions, or lack of them. "We are all responsible for everything that happens to us," Oprah Winfrey once declared, a
statement that might come as a surprise to those who have
landed up in intensive care because a drunken truck driver ran
them down.

Puritanical societies do not simply censure and rebuke, but
sometimes appear to take a grisly delight in doing so. Police officers who force detained Mexican immigrants to wear pink
underclothing in order to humiliate them are not being tough
but just; they are revelling in the obscene pleasures of the sadistic superego. Many Europeans find American prison sentences
grotesquely excessive, and are astonished by the way that twenty
police vehicles with all sirens blaring seem necessary to appre-
hend one seventy-year-old shoplifter. The country is plastered
with prohibitions. "No Smoking Within 150 Yards of This
Store" strikes one as gratuitously vindictive, like putting prison-
ers in shackles and bright orange suits when there is not a chance
in hell of their escaping. One can imagine some creative vari-
ants on such warnings: "No Sneezing Within Half a Mile of
This Bus Stop," for example. There are signs at airports forbid-

ding passengers to make jokes about security matters, including, on occasion, jokes about the notice itself. But what about jokes about jokes about the notice?

Law and religion are here at one. The stout Protestant assumption behind this battery of signs is that human beings are corrupt; that they will therefore do anything outrageously anti-social they can get away with; and that every conceivable kind of transgression, however improbable or bizarre, must be assiduously anticipated and headed off. "Do Not Feed These Cyanide Tablets to Your Toddler." "Do Not Eat This Fire Hydrant." "Do Not Bite the Flight Attendant." "All Passengers Must Be in Possession of a Dormouse." "This program contains images of naked geese: viewer discretion is advised." "Eating this chocolate can cause instant death, incurable bowel disease or make your legs fall off." There is a sign to be found in Britain which reads "Refuse to be Put in This Basket," which seems equally gratuitous until one realises that one is supposed to stress the first syllable of "Refuse." British flight attendants warn you not to tamper with the smoke detectors in the aircraft toilets, whereas American flight attendants warn you not to tamper with, disable or destroy them. If all angles were not covered in this paranoid fashion, some devious American lawyer might no doubt claim that you tampered with the device but did not disable it, or disabled it but did not destroy it. It is no wonder that Henry James heard what he called "the warning moral voice" in everything Emerson wrote.

Since 9/11, the United States has had good reason to worry about security. Even so, it is hard not to feel that it has gone over the top, as it does on so many issues. America is a country where it is difficult to do things by halves. Some people are surreally fat, while others are life-threateningly thin. Some can think of nothing but sex, while others seem to regard sex as more reprehensible than genocide. Some right-wingers are not just conservatives but dangerous lunatics who should not be allowed out without a keeper. Those who believe in cutting food stamps for the poor rather than raising taxes on the owners of private jets are as much in the grip of fanatical dogma as the Muslim terrorists they would love to see burning in hell. It is ironic that the United States is now faced with attacks from fanatical fundamentalists, since there is no shortage of such creatures within its own borders. East coast liberals look anxiously out to the Middle East, alarmed by the bigotry of some of its citizens. They should take a wary glance behind them as well. It is true that most American rednecks are not intent on smashing aircraft into buildings. But a handful of them are preparing for a bloody seizure of power should the nation lapse even more deeply into revolutionary socialism than it has already.

Given its religious and political history, belief in the States plays a more prominent public role than it usually does in advanced capitalist nations. Many such nations believe as little as they can decently get away with. Doctrines are regarded as a hangover from earlier times. It is not belief that holds Finland or South Korea together. It is not what holds the United States together either, but for historical reasons it is mightily more important there. Given this centrality, beliefs are more easily pressed to an extreme. Such extremism is apparent even in fairly trifling matters. Rather than just objecting to other people smoking, some Americans feel compelled to knock their cigarettes violently out of their hands. People do not just rise early, they rise ludicrously, eye-wateringly early.

Excessive zeal also applies to homeland security. Whenever you visit the States these days, you require a new photograph of yourself if the last one you submitted was taken over six months previously. It is just possible that one's hair might have grown down to one's knees in that period, or that one's nose might have mysteriously morphed from bulbous to aquiline. Perhaps American eyes change colour more often than they do in the rest of the world. On submitting a new photo of myself to the U.S. Embassy in Dublin, I once ventured to joke that my fingerprints, too, might have altered out of all recognition over the previous six months, and that they might wish to take them again. They did not seem to find this amusing. On the contrary, they wrote a small note on my file, which was already alarmingly thick. In American airports, one's boarding pass seems to be checked every three or four minutes, as though one's identity might have altered in the process of walking from security to the departure gate.

Law and the Irish

The American cult of prohibition would not go down well in Ireland, a nation where there are plenty of laws but where citizens exercise a degree of individual judgement about which ones to obey. Plainly ridiculous prohibitions, such as not spitting on the sidewalk or not racing your bicycle at high speed through a crowded shopping mall, will simply be ignored. Irish attitudes to the law are shaped by the fact that for many centuries, the justice system in the country was not their own but a colonial imposition. This is an excellent excuse for parking your car in someone's front garden. People who shoplift iPods are really victims of colonial oppression. They might even get round to using this defence in court.

The Irish are a Catholic nation, not a Puritan one. They can be sternly repressive about sex, but much of this dates from the Great Famine, when questions of fertility control, population growth, celibacy, emigration, the division of the land and the like began to bulk large. For the most part, the Irish are not an easily shockable people. One can make outrageous remarks about sex, though not necessarily demeaning comments about the Virgin Mary. In some parts of Protestant Britain, the opposite is true. Morally speaking, they are a remarkably tolerant people. On the whole, the Irish are a moral nation (very few of them get murdered, for example), but not, like a lot of Americans, moralistic. The vigilante spirit is largely foreign to the country, though the Irish have shown themselves well capable of racism in recent times. Even so, it would never occur to them to form a posse to drive prostitutes (as opposed to drug dealers) out of town.

The Irish have also been wary of the Protestant work ethic, which is not a fancy way of suggesting that they are bone idle. This, too, can mark them out from the work-hungry Americans. Irish labourers sweated blood to build the roads and canals of Britain, a country that had helped to despatch many thousands of their compatriots to their graves in the Famine years. Yet they managed for the most part to keep work in proper perspective, and knew that enjoying yourself is morally speaking a good deal more important. Planting potatoes, the traditional economic activity of the Irish, leaves you with a fair amount of leisure, as potatoes generally look after themselves. The Irish thus had time for their feast days and holidays, and devoted large amounts of energy to socialising, as well as to creeping out at night to take pot shots at landlords to whom they might deliver solemn pledges of loyalty during the day.

Nor are the Irish earnest and high-minded. On the contrary, they can be witty, irreverent, satirical and iconoclastic, which is not on the whole true of the inhabitants of Holland, Michigan, or Provo, Utah. They are also deeply unsentimental and have a keen sense of the ridiculous, which is also not generally the case in Holland or Provo. Drinking, dancing, cursing and gambling are not only tolerated in Ireland but sometimes compulsory. Religion there is not notably at odds with gratification. It is true that there have been plenty of Irish kill-joys. A nineteenth-century bishop once remarked that Irish dancing was morally speaking the best kind of dancing there was. He meant that there could be no groping, since Irish dancing involves holding your arms by your sides. He also meant that it is so exhausting that it leaves little energy for any more dubious acts of pleasure. Even so, English visitors to Ireland in the eighteenth century could be scandalised by the free sexual talk of the young women, which did not of course imply that they were sexually free in reality.

Intolerance and Public Spirit

Religious civilisations are often thought to be intolerant ones. When it comes to the United States, the answer to the question of whether it is a tolerant or intolerant nation is a decisive yes. Purple-faced bigots are allowed to gather on street corners to bawl their hatred of those with views different from their own. This is an excellent thing. And an appalling one too, of course.

In some ways, the country is magnificent about allowing people to do their own thing. In other ways, its visceral resistance to anything that differs from it is legendary. A recent poll revealed that one in five Alabamians and more than one in four Mississippians believe interracial marriage should be illegal. Americans are allowed to go to all kinds of eccentric lengths to make money, but are expected on the whole to conform to small-town mores in the process. Flamboyance is acceptable, but not outright aberration. De Tocqueville thought America had less freedom of discussion and independence of mind than any other nation. Freedom of spirit, he writes, is unknown there. Since freedom of spirit is exactly what the United States prides itself on, this is rather like complaining that the Italians can't sing and the French have nothing worth eating. De Tocqueville's complaint is certainly not true of the United States today, where there is an impressive amount of spiritual free enterprise.

The tyranny of public opinion is what most disturbed this European observer about the country. You were not exactly coerced, but you were not exactly free either. The irony of democracy for de Tocqueville is that it substitutes the voice of the people for political despotism, but that voice can be as stifling and oppressive as a Sultan's. It is thus that political freedom gives birth to its opposite. You can believe what you like, he remarks, but if it fails to chime with the opinions of your neighbours, they will treat you as a pariah. Nobody, he adds, is prevented from writing licentious books, but nobody would think of doing so either.

Writing licentious books aside, there is still something of this moral climate in the States today. It is never entirely safe to demonstrate in the name of a deeply unpopular cause on the streets of Britain, but it is probably safer than doing so in many an American town. All the same, de Tocqueville's remarks grossly underestimate the range and diversity of American freedoms. It is true that you can allow people all the liberty you like once you know that they have internalised all the proper restraints. But the United States, like Europe, remains a place where you cannot be carted off to prison for declaring your allegiance to Rosa Luxemburg. This is not a freedom to be underrated. There are those elsewhere in the world who have given their lives to attain it. The only problem is that it is shrinking all the time, as state surveillance and the spectre of Islamism loom larger.

Religion in America goes hand in hand with a strong civic spirit. It is a more Victorian society than Britain in several ways, not least in its cult of philanthropy. Most British students would not care to depend for their labs and dorms on the charitable whims of millionaire businessmen in pursuit of tax breaks. They would want this no more than they would wish to see Prince Charles handing out food parcels to the deserving poor in Trafalgar Square. They regard education as a right, not a privilege. In fact, most British students would like to see college education free of charge, funded perhaps by the tens of billions of pounds lost to the country each year in tax evasion.

Even so, the mighty lineage of American philanthropy reflects the nation's civic conscience, which is a great deal more vigorous than it is across the Atlantic. Public-spiritedness is a resplendent American virtue. In his *American Notes*, Charles Dickens reserves some of his most rhapsodic prose for the civic life of Boston. "Above all," he writes in florid vein, "I sincerely believe that the public institutions and charities of this capital of Massachusetts are as nearly perfect, as the most considerate wisdom, benevolence, and humanity, can make them. I never in my life was more affected by the contemplation of happiness, under circumstances of privation and bereavement, than in my visits to these establishments." He is speaking of such places as the Boston asylum for the blind and hospital for the insane, and is rather keener on these institutions than he is on the Washington Senate. The Senate is, he allows, "a dignified and decorous body," but one whose dignity is somewhat tarnished by the state to which the carpets have been reduced "by the universal disregard of the spittoon." He also notes the curiously swollen faces of some of its members, "caused by the quantity of tobacco they contrive to stow within the hollow of the cheek." U.S. senators who were caught stashing tobacco in their cheeks today would probably be forced to spend the rest of their lives hiding out in the Nevada desert. It might be better for them to be caught illicitly consorting with a donkey.

Anarchy, Law, and Eccentricity

Puritan cultures can be both repressive and individualist. No doubt this is one reason why the United States is such an odd combination of anarchy and authoritarianism. This is not as surprising a mixture as it may seem. If everybody is allowed to do their own thing, you need a particularly stout framework of order with which to contain this potential chaos. Things are rather different in the United Kingdom. The British are a largely law-abiding bunch, but they also have a streak of libertarianism. So do Americans—but whereas in the States this tends to be an ideological affair, complete with high-pitched rhetoric about the dangers of state control, it is a less political matter in Britain. The British dislike authority not because they are opposed to the state on principle, but because they want to be left alone to breed pigeons or attend classes in flower arranging. They do not want to be free of regulation so that they can aspire, rise through the ranks or accumulate profit, but so that they can potter about as they please. They are not so much individualist as idiosyncratic. Their resentment of those in charge is less politically militant than passive-aggressive. It is part of the "free-born Englishman" syndrome, which is less strident and self-conscious than the "free American" complex.

The British want to be allowed to pursue their own quirky way of life with as little interference from others as possible. This differs from American libertarianism, with its fear that a sinisterly autocratic state will rob citizens of their initiative and autonomy. On this view, the British National Health Service is a place where you describe your medical symptoms to a robot cunningly disguised as a physician, which then relays them to an underground bunker in Whitehall where a computer the size of an aircraft carrier decides whether you should be treated or painlessly put down. Cancer patients might find that the funds for their treatment are suddenly withdrawn in order to fund the repair of potholes on the M6 motorway.

It is not the state that the British object to, but other people. Not long ago, the most popular sport in the United Kingdom was not soccer but fishing. Fishing is a fine excuse for avoiding other people. The same is true of the collegiate system at Oxford and Cambridge. Because everyday life in these universities is organised on a collegiate rather than departmental basis, you do not have to encounter other people in your own academic subject from one year's end to another. This is one of the great advantages of having a job in these places, and ought to be emphasised in their advertising. Since the person sitting next to you at college lunch is likely to be in a subject you have never heard of, let alone know anything about, there is no tedious necessity to talk to them. This greatly enhances the quality of intellectual life, as with those marriages in which one partner lives in San Diego and the other in Hong Kong. The durability of such relationships tends to restore one's faith in wedlock.

Over the centuries, the British have perfected all kinds of ingenious methods for avoiding each other. Americans, by contrast, are a gregarious crowd, endlessly clubbable. The country is stuffed with guilds, fraternities, sororities, learned societies and professional associations, along with conferences, seminars, conventions, summer institutes and other such anthropological rituals, all of which are taken with immense seriousness. One of the largest of such bashes is the annual convention of the Modern Language Association, where it is possible to be in hotels with thousands of other people all of whom could tell you the name of Hamlet's mother. People in Britain attend such gatherings less frequently and eagerly, and do so largely in order to drink. They are shy creatures, not easily taken into captivity. Life is so arranged as to avoid as far as possible those unfortunate collisions known as meeting other people.

The British, then, are out to protect their divine right to be eccentric, not to voice some aggressively libertarian doctrine. They are quite willing to accept authority provided it does not disrupt their way of life. When it does, they become bloody-minded, which is not a word generally familiar to Americans. To be bloody-minded means not to throw up barricades in the streets but to be doggedly, persistently, perversely non-cooperative. The British have a special affection for people who are cussed, cross-grained and curmudgeonly. It is an echo of their Nonconformist past. The icon of British liberty is the citizen who causes a motorway to be re-routed because he will not give up his one-acre vegetable patch. This, not someone who jumps off a bridge to save a drowning child, is the British definition of a hero. The other kind of hero in Britain is someone who jumps off a bridge to save a drowning dog.

The well-regulated nature of American life goes hand in hand with its moralistic outlook. Compared with the Irish, Americans are by and large a judgemental people. There is a good deal of sermonising and sententiousness. A certain self-righteousness is never far from the American soul. So-called interventions are not unknown, in which the whole of one's extended family, along with several busloads of friends, colleagues, acquaintances, and random strangers along for the ride, break down your front door and spill into your living room to warn you of the perils of smoking the occasional after-dinner cigar.

This would never happen in Britain. Instead, the British would allow you to die in the gutter, pustular and emaciated, for fear of interfering with your privacy. They would let you perish friendless and unaided for roughly the same reasons they would not dream of speaking to you in a railway compartment. It is not that they are hard-hearted, just that they believe in minding their own business. Their ethic of live-and-let-live can escalate to lethal extremes. They go to extraordinary efforts to pretend that other people are not there, like men and women under hypnosis whose fingernails are being pulled out by a pair of pliers but who do not react because they have been told that they are alone.

The Affirmative Spirit

Comedy and Compromise

The story is told in Ireland of a fiddlers' competition out in the west, the winner of which would become All-Ireland champion. (The title "All-Ireland champion" is admittedly rather loose: one tends to bump into scores of All-Irish champion musicians up and down the country, as though every second woman on the street in the United States were to turn out to be Miss America.) The first contender for the award stepped on to the stage: a suave, distinguished-looking, silver-haired gentleman in evening dress, exquisitely coifed and bearing in his hand a genuine Stradivarius. Resting the instrument against his chin with a well-practised flourish, he drew the bow vigorously across the strings and began to play.

And by God he was useless.

The second candidate for stardom then turned to face the audience—a slick-haired, flashy-toothed type in a well-tailored grey suit, carrying in his hand an expensive but not classic violin. With an ingratiating smile, he placed the instrument under his chin and began to play.

And by God he was useless.

The judges were just on the point of declaring a no-winner when there was a slight commotion at the back of the room. Despite his evident reluctance, a third competitor was being forced to the front by his friends—a tiny, shrunken, octogenarian fellow in a crumpled old suit buttoned up with bits of string and hardly a seat to his trousers. In his withered claw lay a fiddle as decrepit as himself, its strings frayed and peeling, its wood leashed together by elastic bands. Shrinking from the crowd, but urged on loyally by his friends, he placed the fiddle beneath his chin with a quivering hand and softly drew the tattered bow across it.

And by God he was useless too.

There is a sense in which this is an anti-American story. For one thing, it represents a smack in the face for sentimentalists, of whom there are a good many in the United States. For another thing, it appeals to populist feelings only to deflate them. It panders to the champions of the Common Man, then turns on them with its last breath and leaves them disconcerted. Like a good deal in Irish culture, it builds up lofty expectations only to undercut them. It is also typical of that culture in its perversity. It promises to gratify our desire for a conventional upbeat ending, then pulls the rug out sadistically from under our feet. It trades on our liberal-minded assumption that appearances are no sure guide to reality, only to reveal that the fiddler is every bit as inept as he looks. Like a lot of Irish humour, the story is latently aggressive. It represents the revenge of those with a secret grudge against self-satisfied, smoothly predictable narratives. In typically Irish vein, it is about failure, not success, and failure as comic rather than as tragic.

Rather as the Irishman Oscar Wilde's epigrams take a conventional piece of English wisdom and rip it inside out or stand it on its head, so this tale takes the traditional fairy story in which the beggar becomes king and leaves him even more of a loser than he was in the first place. In all these ways, the fable resembles not the humour of Americans in general but of American Jews in particular. It is not for nothing that the hero of the finest Irish novel ever written, James Joyce's *Ulysses*, is called Bloom. The fiddler joke works by bathos, one of the most typical of Irish literary devices. Hacking the world savagely down to size is a familiar Irish pastime. Deflation and debunkery are among the nation's favourite pursuits. In this, Irish culture is very different in sensibility from the United States, which has been so generous to the country over the centuries. Debunkery is too negative an act for many Americans to feel easy about.

The Irish can be negative in the sense of satirical, but not in the sense of complaining too bitterly when things go wrong. This is partly because they live in a country which within living memory hovered somewhere between first and third worlds, and which has recently tipped back towards third-world status again. Life is thus not expected to be highly streamlined. Transport timetables, for example, are sometimes largely decorative, with only a loose relationship to observable fact. But the Irish reluctance to complain is also because it is imprudent to stand out as a trouble-maker in a small country where everyone knows everyone else. The British complain rather more, and have much to complain about; but they do so in a muttering, shamefaced sort of way, in case other people might complain in a muttering, shamefaced sort of way about their complaining.

Both comedy and tragedy are about coming unstuck. The difference lies in the way we respond to this debacle. Comedy is the art form which understands that coming unstuck is fairly commonplace. It is part of everyday existence to trip over your own feet from time to time, to fall apart at the seams, or fail to live up to your own grandiose ideals. If you do not aspire too high or expect too much, however, you will never have far to tumble, and will never be too crestfallen. By keeping your head down, refusing the seductions of greatness, you can survive. You will never be a saint or a conqueror, but your failures will be minor ones. In classical tragedy, those who aspire and fall make more of a splash because they tend to be privileged, heroic types. Comedy, by contrast, is the anti-heroic mode of those who accept the inevitability of things going awry, and have learnt to be stoical about it. It avoids the afflictions of tragedy by sacrificing its splendour. Comedy settles for half, tolerant and disenchanted, sceptical of all wide-eyed idealism and passionate intensity, adept at the art of compromise. It is not a cynical form, since it believes in the reality of human value; but it believes that such value is best preserved by not making too much of a fuss about it. It is a very British way of seeing.

Like comedy, the British are traditionally suspicious of the success ethic. Unlike Americans, they are not an affirmative nation. Among their national icons are a ship that sank (the *Titanic*) and a calamitous military defeat (Dunkirk). Defeat is what the British are particularly good at. They are maestros of utter disaster. No doubt there are bunkers deep below Whitehall where intensive seminars in how to screw up are secretly conducted. Glorious defeats, like the Charge of the Light Brigade, are almost to be elevated over stupendous victories. The British are not proactively heroic, but brave out of necessity. Unlike Americans, the only kind of heroism for which they have a sneaking admiration is one forced on you when the odds are hopeless and your back is to the wall. After such sporadic bursts of self-sacrificial glory, they resume their normal, grumpy, unheroic existence until the next catastrophe happens along. They need the occasional hardship in order to show what stuff they are made of, and suspect that American civilisation is too easy and flaccid in this respect. The States may be full of virile, chiseljawed, bestubbled types, but all those stretch limos and Jacuzzis are fatally weakening. This is ironic, since quite a few Americans see the British themselves as effete. This is largely because their accents can sound vaguely gay, rather like their prose styles.

The British are no enthusiasts of extremes. They are not convinced that truth is what shines forth when you are driven to the outer edge. This can happen from time to time, as when German submarines are sinking your supply ships, but it is out of the ordinary. It should not be taken as a measure by which to characterise everyday life. The real self is the everyday, middle-of-the-road one. It is one that lends itself to the novel, a form at which the British have been adept, rather than to epic or tragedy. The British value freedom, for example, but tend to suspect that Americans make too much of a song and dance about it. Charles Dickens records in his *American Notes* an encounter he had with a doctor who insists he has no intention of leaving America. "Not yet awhile, Sir, not yet. You won't catch me at that just yet, Sir. I am a little too fond of freedom for *that*, Sir. Ha, ha! It's not so easy for a man to tear himself away from a free country such as this is, Sir! Ha, ha! No, no! Ha, ha! None of that, till one's obliged to do it, Sir. No, no." The doctor turns out to be a Scot who has only been in the country for three or four months. The national rhetoric is clearly contagious.

The middle of the road can be a dangerous place to stand. You are likely to get run over from both directions. It can also be an illusion. What is the middle way between racism and anti-racism, or tickling someone as opposed to torturing them? Even so, middle-of-the-roadism, which in Britain is almost as much an object of veneration as Manchester United, is probably less perilous than the sharper kinds of polarity one finds in the United States. Good guys and bad guys, for example. There are, in fact, no entirely good guys, which is not to say that there are no saints. It is just that saints are by no means entirely good guys. The Catholic Church allows that even they can have bouts of wrath and twinges of lust. Perhaps there are no completely bad guys either. Even monstrous despots weep over their sick children. The British believe that life is mixed and muddled, a view of the world that is exemplified by their weather. It is a supreme example of the pied and dappled nature of things, their chanciness and unpredictability, the way you can never really trust life when it is running smoothly because sunshine turns so often to showers. It is a metaphor for the nation's mentality.

The British are fond of sayings like "It takes all kinds to make a world," "There's a bit of good and bad in everybody," and "It would be a funny world if we all thought the same." Fist fights can sometimes be avoided by telling your opponent that he has a right to his opinion and you have a right to yours. It is surprising how often this piece of threadbare liberal wisdom can prevent a punch in the face. It works partly by implying that people should leave each other alone, which the British are usually delighted to do. The British "muddle through," meaning that they achieve their goals but don't quite know how, and might just as easily not have done. The role of accident and approximation in human affairs is ruefully acknowledged. Things in the States are more conscious and clear-cut, rather like the layout of some of its cities. The aim is less compromise than achievement, so that you hatch your plan and put it efficiently into operation. The only problem with this is even if you do not mess it up, reality will probably do so for you. Such, at least, is the view of life across the Atlantic.

Grumbling and Grousing

The fact that the British are always grousing might suggest that they are gripped by a dream of perfection. But this is not so. They grouse largely because they enjoy doing so, and would be at a loss if their complaints were all to be satisfied. One reason why they talk about the weather so much is that it is often pretty bad, a fact from which, as chronic masochists, they reap a morose kind of pleasure. It also allows them to grumble without getting too personal in their protests, thus risking a broken rib. Since nobody is likely to take a bitter harangue about hailstones personally, one can vent one's spleen without fear of being physically assaulted. The subject also appeals to the deep-seated fatalism of the British people, since there is no way of stopping a thunderstorm. This, too, is a secret source of self-lacerating joy among the citizenry. The British rather enjoy feeling helpless, as the Americans do not. The thought that there is absolutely nothing one can do is regarded by some in the United States as defeatist, nihilistic and in some obscure sense unpatriotic. In Britain, it brings with it a strange, luminous, semi-mystical kind of peace.

It is important to note that the British do not just complain about the weather when it is cold and damp. They complain about it when it is hot and dry as well. In their view, too much sunshine is almost as offensive as a tsunami. The British are not in general prima donnas, and tend to disapprove of any such capricious behaviour. When it comes to the weather, however, they can no more be satisfied than a pampered rock star who smashes the bottles of Moët & Chandon champagne backstage because he asked for apple juice. The weather, like seaside holidays and overseas football matches, is Britain's occasion for infantile self-indulgence.

Another reason why the British talk about the weather so much is that it is one of the few things common to everyone in a socially divided nation. It is also because the weather in Britain is perpetually changing and wildly unpredictable, and thus lends itself to animated discussion rather more than the unwavering heat of the Sahara. Along with illness, it is one of the few dramatic aspects of everyday life. If the country were blessed with a calculable climate, its citizens would be struck dumb. Talking about rain and fog, however, is also a way of avoiding talking about more intimate matters, of which the British are notably shy. (So, indeed, are the Irish, who seem more frank and open than their former proprietors but who have all sorts of secret depths.) Sex as a topic of conversation is of general interest but too revealing, while the demography of sixteenth-century Portugal is unrevealing but not of general interest. So storm clouds and regions of low pressure must serve instead.

Grumbling in Britain is a mild form of social dissidence. It is a way of rebelling against the current order of things without the bother of having to do anything about it, thus blunting the edge of one's protest with a very British stoicism. It also involves a kind of negative solidarity: one grouses to others who in turn bellyache back, in an anthropological ritual whose gambits and conventions are intuitively understood. Discussing one's physical ailments in gruesome detail, another time-honoured British pastime, is a similar form of negative solidarity. People take it for granted that doctors are useless and hospitals criminally incompetent, and compete with each other to produce the most blood-chilling medical anecdotes. Accidental amputations, hearts removed but not replaced, eyes left dangling on cheeks, cell phones, pork pies and cigarette lighters sewn up inside patients by mistake: all have been known to figure in this lugubrious one-upmanship. You can be obsessed with illness, however, without being neurotic about it, as some Americans are. The British assume that the body will break down from time to time, and would feel deprived of an agreeable topic of conversation if it did not. A super-efficient health service would plunder the nation of precious grumbling resources, thus leaving people with a lot less to say to each other. Contracting syphilis may be the only way to get to know the people next door.

Many of the British have an unerring conviction that the future will be different from the present, namely, worse. There are always fresh catastrophes just round the corner. For some

Americans, there is also an unimaginable catastrophe just round the corner, but it is known as the Apocalypse and will have a positive outcome, at least for those who believe in it. Even the end of the world is not the end of the world. Some British attitudes to the future could be described as apocalypticism without the religion. History has been in steep decline ever since some indeterminate golden age. The nation's best days have always gone. To adopt a phrase of Oscar Wilde's, the British have a great future behind them. Even the golden age was not all it is cracked up to be. Even then, people glanced back nostalgically to some previous paradise. And even in Eden there was a snake in the garden. In the States, by contrast, one frequently hears that the nation's best days lie ahead of it. In fact, this has probably been a constant refrain since the Pilgrim Fathers. It tacitly acknowledges that the present is not exactly brilliant, but does so in a way that avoids dwelling too despondently on the fact.

The attitude of the stereotypical British workman illustrates the nation's generic glumness. Confronted with a blocked pipe or a broken radiator, he will stare at it in gloomy silence for several minutes, hand on hips, shake his head slowly and finally come out with a deep-throated "Nah." There is, he will imply with funereal satisfaction, absolutely no way in which this disaster can be repaired. After a lengthy period of anxious questioning, in which one is obliged to participate as in some vital ritual at a voodoo ceremony, he will grudgingly admit that there might just be a way of fixing the problem, though it will be fiendishly complicated and insanely expensive. Ten minutes later, the repair will be complete, a modest amount of money will have changed hands, and the workman will have moved on to another bout of Nah-ing and head-shaking elsewhere.

Nothing could be further from everyday America. The United States is a land where for the most part things work. It is streamlined, efficient, labour-saving and economical. Service in bars and restaurants is prompt, cheerful and efficient. In Europe, by contrast, waiters can go to extraordinarily ingenious lengths to avoid serving you. One suspects they engage in competitions with each other over who can delay delivering food the longest. When they finally appear with your meal, they sometimes look rather older than they did when you ordered it. Efficient service is not a British priority. Indeed, in some pubs and cafés it is regarded as a kind of moral defect. I once knew a Manchester bus driver who devoted his life to seeing how many people he could leave behind at bus stops. He was inordinately proud of this achievement. When I caught sight of him across a crowded pub, he would gleefully hold up a number of fingers to indicate the latest toll of abandoned passengers. British workers do not typically take pride in the outfits that employ them. Not many of them would refer to their companies as "we," as American workers tend to do. Attempts to induce them to identify with the company as a whole might be greeted with ridicule. They are not especially impressed by Employee of the Month schemes, or chief executives who wear "Rage Against the Machine" T-shirts and ask to be called Sweetie Pie.

Failure and Success

Unlike the British, Americans do not generally take a doleful delight in breakdown and failure. This is because they are trained to admire achievement. They can thus be less envious and begrudging than those for whom good fortune is as rare as humility in Hollywood. At the same time, societies like the United States which insist on success are bound to produce large amounts of human wreckage. This, however, has been efficiently taken into account. There is a dynamic, fabulously profitable machine for mopping the damage up, all the way from psychotherapy to the churches, mystic mud baths to Indian healing rituals. One part of the system reduces people to burnt-out shells by seeking to pump too much profit out of them, while the other part reaps a profit out of trying to stitch them together again.

The behaviour of a nation is influenced by how big it is. When it comes to a civilisation, size matters. One can speak freely of one's triumphs in the States because success is generally applauded, but also because there are so many Americans that a lot of other people are likely to have chalked up achievements as well, and envy is thus less of a problem. In small nations like Ireland or Norway, backbiting and resentment are rife, since there are not enough people around for many of them to stand out as exceptional. The few who do excel are thus at dire risk of being cut briskly down to size. Egalitarianism in the States is a virtue, and so it is in Sweden, but in smaller societies it can be a negative value as well. It means that nobody should have the nerve to get above anybody else. Getting on is regarded as rather suspect, and if you are ill-starred enough to be a billionaire banker or world-class clarinet player you would be well advised to conceal the fact. The more you soar, the more you should keep your head down. The best policy is to rise without trace. Familiarity breeds scepticism: people know their neighbours too well to believe that their good fortune is truly deserved. You should fit in with your fellows, not seek to outshine them.

The British habit is to efface the ego, whereas the American one is to assert it. This, at least, is what the formal ideology of each nation requires, however remote it may be from the behaviour of their citizens. There are plenty of arrogant Brits and self-lacerating Texans. De Tocqueville remarks that Americans have turned egoism into a social and political theory. In Britain, self-effacement is bound up with the ethic of service. You are not to consider your own selfish interests, but to subordinate them to the Crown, the Empire, the defence of the realm or the common good. Those who do so are a privileged elite, and the ethic of service, while real enough in one sense, is also a way of masking this privilege behind a cloak of selflessness.

The aristocrat, rather similarly, justifies his august status by devoting himself to the well-being of his tenants and lackeys. He makes a point of being pleasant to his servants, whereas vulgar upstarts of stockbrokers make a point of being rude to them in order to demonstrate their superiority. Only low-bred types are snobs. The word began as a term for a shoemaker, and was then used to refer to the socially inferior. It meant not upper-class people who despise lower-class ones, but lower-class ones with a grudge against upper-class ones. Because he can do what he pleases, the aristocrat is a kind of anarchist, and thus has more affinity with the poacher than with the gamekeeper. He understands that genuine power does not need to make a display of itself, any more than real men are constantly fretting about their sperm count. True authority is so firmly entrenched that it can take itself for granted, like so many of the things the British regard as precious.

The United States is neither a particularly comic society nor an especially tragic one. It is too affirmative to be tragic, and too

much in love with heroism to be comic. When it comes to affirmation, the can-do spirit is one of the great divides between the
United States and Europe. At my son's American school, there
was a poster on the wall that read "Success Comes in Cans." In
some quarters of the States, the word "can't" seems as offensive
as the word "Communist." Success in the States also comes in
CANIs, which for one American self-help writer means Constant, Never-Ending Improvement. Since there are always more
goals to strive for, what he is in fact promoting is a life of perpetual dissatisfaction.

Failure is not an option, as the typically American word
"challenge" suggests. Being buried up to your neck in excrement
while famished crows peck at your eyeballs is not a problem but
a challenge. "Challenge" suggests that problems exist to test
your mettle, and are thus to be regarded as positive rather than
negative. Problems are not a problem. It is not a problem if
chemical warfare breaks out in Mississippi, but a God-sent
opportunity for you to "come out of it stronger." The current
British equivalent of these pious clichés is "learning lessons,"
which is a coded way of admitting that you have committed
some atrocious blunder. If the police have shot dead a whole
class of kindergarten children under the impression that they
were a gang of armed drug dealers, there are "lessons to be
learnt." The passive voice is compulsory. That you may have
something to learn is the closest you can decently come to apologising in an age when nobody apologises much any more.

Any society which calls its prisons "correctional facilities" is
excessively optimistic. Prison hardly ever corrects anyone.
Wherever possible in the States, you are expected to affirm.
When asked how your holiday was, it is not really done to reply,

"Dreadful." My daughter once attended an American pre-school in which the teachers were trained never to speak negatively to the children. When asked how they responded to bad behaviour, they replied piously, "We don't react." A small boy who was punched in the face by a fellow pupil received the compliment, "Thank you, James, for not reacting." The way to handle trouble, in other words, was to pretend that it wasn't happening. My daughter, being of a mischievous turn of mind, instantly exploited this permissive spirit by letting off all the fire alarms. Her teacher's response was "My, Alice sure loves to learn!" There are other ways to describe the havoc she created.

In one sense, however, this endemic upbeatness is all to no avail. One index of national happiness ranks the United States at a paltry number 150 among the world's nations. Americans are less likely to move upwards from their social class of origin than a whole array of other countries. Since these are discouraging statistics, they are best ignored. Brooding on them will make your hair fall out. In fact, for some Americans this is a genuine risk. Being negative generates vibes which can give you cancer, scupper your chances of financial success, and drive your spouse to commit adultery with a whole soccer team.

Illness, however trivial and curable, is a foretaste of death, and thus a souvenir of our ultimate powerlessness. There are two ways of handling that impotence, the first of which is to repress it. Reminding people that they are frail, vulnerable creatures is not the best way of squeezing a profitable day's work out of them, or having them confront enemy bullets in defence of the realm. The other way is the path of tragedy, which draws its power not from sidestepping human frailty but from confronting and embracing it. It does not regard suffering as positive, any more·

than the New Testament does. Instead, it holds that if one has the misfortune to be visited by some affliction, one must try not to disavow it but to pass all the way through it, in the hope that one might eventually emerge somewhere on the other side. One must try to let go of oneself in the faith that one might find oneself again. This is not the same as seeking out suffering in order to improve your character or enhance your virility. People who do that are not tragic but absurd.

Cultures that can maintain a pact with failure are those than can thrive. Civilisations are to be judged by how far they honour their father and their mother. The Biblical injunction has nothing to do with the family. It had to do in its day with how one treated the old and useless of the tribe, those who were unable to labour. The United States, unlike the writings of Samuel Beckett, is not especially enamoured of pacts with failure. It is a profoundly anti-tragic nation, which has recently lived through one of the darkest episodes of its history. It is besieged by those who feel themselves to be on the sticky end of its formidable power, and who are now striking murderously back. Militarily speaking, the country is superbly well equipped to deal with these dangers. Spiritually speaking, its anti-tragic view of existence leaves it peculiarly disarmed.

Not that the States is without its tragedies. I was once in a bookstore in the Midwest when it was proudly announced over the public address system that the author of a book entitled *Barns of Indiana* was present in the store, and was willing to sign copies of his book. I emerged from around a bookcase to see a small, crumpled, shy-looking man sitting at a table, pen poised hopefully in hand, beside a pile of books that seemed to stretch to the ceiling. Not a soul was within twenty yards of him, though the place was fairly crowded. After lingering in the store for another hour or so, I made my way to the entrance only to catch sight of the author still sitting at his table, visibly more crumpled in appearance, pen still poised, the pile of books still in place, and the area around him still utterly deserted. I turned my back on this poignant sight and strode quickly away. The phrase "Barns of Indiana" is still capable of waking me up at night with a guilty start. In my dreams I rewind the spool of history, return to the bookstore, stride genially up to the little man's table and buy a dozen copies of his book. But the truth is that I shamefully backed off, and will never be able to undo this despicable act.

There is, to be sure, a positive side to American starry-eyedness. In the end, what matters in human affairs is not optimism or pessimism but realism, and it is sometimes realistic to be hopeful. Hope is not necessarily naive, and Americans are indeed superb at problem-solving. They are resourceful, ingenious, inventive and constructive. It is just that you can be all these excellent things without suppressing the truth that all human beings finally come to utter ruin. In fact, these virtues are all the more commendable if you can practice them while staring failure candidly in the face. Otherwise one buys one's cheerfulness on the cheap. The early American Puritans were aware that a virtue which does not wrestle with negativity is worthless.

What one might call pathological optimism is actually a form of weakness, despite its square-jawed grin and steady gaze. It reflects a fear of confronting loss, and loss is far more central to being human than accomplishment. As such, it is just as unrealistic as the professional pessimism of so many of the British, for whom gloom is a kind of religious obligation. Americans keen on self-motivation are warned by specialists in the field who visit their companies not to read newspapers or watch TV news because of their negative content. Thinking about the slums of Mumbai might ruin their chances of a raise. Because there is not much they can do about famine in Ethiopia, such events are offensive to the cult of the will. Optimism of this kind is as much a disavowal of reality as psychosis, if somewhat less spectacular. The United States has disastrously failed to exploit the power of negative thinking. It has refused to take the point of Bertolt Brecht's dictum: "Scepticism can move mountains."

The British, by contrast, have no such credulous trust in the magic of the mind. They are unwavering in their assurance that problems, like sin for Evangelicals or alcohol for the AA, are phenomena in the face of which we are entirely helpless. If an American and a Briton were together in a prisoner-of-war camp, the Briton would fade gradually away with a plucky little grin and the American would escape. There are, of course, plenty of Americans who refuse the lie of the omnipotent will. If there is the general's view of how the war is going, there is also that of the medical orderly who has to mop up the blood. Working people, for example, tend to be more realistic than their superiors, since they are closer to the ground. For those further from the facts, optimism is easy, but realism is fatiguingly hard.

One reason why Americans are encouraged to be hopeful is that gloom is felt to be politically subversive. In this, too, the United States is a thoroughly Victorian kind of place. Victorian novels were not really allowed to end badly. The point of art was to cheer you up. Pessimism and socialism went hand in hand. Miserable people are likely to be socially disaffected. You therefore need either to get them to grin, or to deepen their misery to the point where they are too depleted and demoralised to do anything about it. People who are both powerful and dissatisfied are peculiarly dangerous. In general, cheerfulness is on the side of the status quo. The battle between the left and the right is among other things one between satire on the one hand, and good, clean, wholesome humour on the other. Good, clean, wholesome humorists tend to find satire nihilistic, and irritably inquire what one proposes to put in place of whatever is under fire. Bad, unclean, unwholesome humorists should resist this moral blackmail. Satire may be negative in content, but it is supremely positive in form. There is no criticism, however scabrous, that does not implicitly subscribe to an alternative vision of things.

The belief that you can change the world by positive thinking is a kind of magic. It is the sort of faith one imagines an infant might have. Perhaps there is a touch of such magic in the cult of political correctness, for which to purge language is to purify reality. If you cannot get rid of racial inequality for real, you can always do so vicariously by changing the way you talk. This is not to suggest that speech and thought are unimportant. Europeans tend to see optimism and pessimism as ways of judging situations, whereas Americans see them as ways of creating them. If you are too despondent about your prospects, you are unlikely to succeed. People who are sour and snappish because they have no friends are unlikely to have any friends. Optimism, on the other hand, is a force which can fashion what you desire, rather like a wizard's wand. Cheerful people are more likely to be successful than despondent ones because of the way other people treat them, though they also seem a lot more likely to end up murdered. News reports almost always describe the youthful victims of homicidal maniacs as having been zestful, bubbly, fun-loving people with hordes of friends and a great future ahead of them. Miserable people rarely get murdered.

In this sense, both optimism and pessimism can be self-validating. For Americans, they are ways of doing something, not just ways of describing something. Not to have what you want is a problem, but it is also a sort of solution, since to feel your lack keenly enough is to be moved to get what you desire. Perhaps this is what Marx had in mind when he wrote that humankind sets itself only such problems as it can solve. Hope is a self-fulfilling prophecy. There is a grain of truth in this, along with a heap of delusion. Feeling hopeful is not going to catapult a destitute drug addict into the White House, though it might help to send a rich, reformed one there. Besides, if a destitute drug addict feels good about himself, then he shouldn't. To feel satisfied with himself is to do himself an injustice, just as he would if his life was faring magnificently but he continually put himself down. People who feel bad about themselves may be eminently rational in their self-estimation. They should not be persuaded out of it by a lot of consoling lies.

For some Americans, feeling good about yourself is a sacred duty, like placing your hand on your heart at certain patriotic moments. "I weigh four hundred pounds, smoke four packs a day and have just taken a machete to all three of my kids, but I still feel good about myself" is the kind of declaration that might win you a spontaneous burst of applause on certain American TV shows. One of the problems with the country is that not enough people feel bad about themselves. Too many people believe in themselves on palpably insufficient evidence, rather as too many people believe in guardian angels on similarly slender grounds.

For every sufferer from low self-esteem who needs cuddling, there is a megalomaniac who needs kicking. De Tocqueville thought that Americans were "in a state of perpetual self-adoration," and had constantly to be flattered. "No [American] writer," he comments, "no matter how famous, can escape from the obligation to sprinkle incense over his fellow citizens." "Self-adoration" is far too strong, and Americans today can be as open to criticism as anyone else; but the cult of self-belief still strikes one as excessive. You can buy a wheeled suitcase in the States inscribed with your name and Web site in large letters, so as to market yourself while strolling through public places. Someone might always step up, impressed by your chutzpah, and invite you to become president of United Artists.

There is, however, a price to be paid for the success ethic. A recent study showed that rich Americans tend to be more selfish and less empathetic than the poor. Compassion is for the most part a working-class virtue, not an upper-class one. Working people respond much more strongly to images of starving children that rich people do. This is gravely embarrassing for the political left. For years, they have been at pains to point out that the self-interest they deplore is a social question rather than an individual one. It is a whole class they are criticising, not this or that banker or industrialist, who can no doubt be as soft-hearted as Santa Claus. It is not personal greed that drives the system, but the need to amass profit in order to stay competitive, a need which is as impersonal as moonlight. It now turns out that this case was far too sophisticated, and that images of the wicked, top-hatted, lip-curling capitalist have much to be said for them.

It is not true that what you feel is what you are. Donald Trump, for example, clearly feels that he is an astonishing success as a human being. In any case, this is to assume that we can always be sure of what we are feeling, which is far from true. I may have no idea what I am feeling, or imagine that I am feeling angry when in fact I am afraid. You may be able to describe my emotional state far better than I can. The belief that how you feel is how you are assumes that we are always transparent to ourselves and never self-deceived. Nobody could ever surprise me by telling me that I am thoroughly miserable. On this theory, I am in full possession of my own experience, as I am in full possession of my Bermuda shorts.

The theory also assumes that happiness is a state of mind rather than a condition of being. A galley slave who can look forward to another forty years of rowing sixteen hours a day, while being lashed every fifteen minutes, cannot be happy even though he might think he is. To call himself happy simply goes to show that he does not know how to apply the word appropriately, perhaps because he has never been able to contrast his current situation with one of true content. Happiness for Aristotle, as for Hegel and Marx, is a matter of flourishing, which in turn is a question of how far you can freely realise your powers as enjoyable ends in themselves. You may think you are doing this, but you may be mistaken. You may not be in the right social circumstances to do so.

The Rhetoric of Hope

The upbeat mood of America goes hand in hand with the explicitness of its ideology. To keep the nation on its toes, you need to keep reminding it of its dynamism and special destiny.

The right to bear arms, for example, must be proclaimed from the roof tops, though some scholars now consider that this is a misreading of the American Constitution. What it actually guarantees is the right to *bare arms*, but a smudge on the original manuscript has obscured this fact. The British tend to see this ideological upfrontness more as a sign of anxiety than assurance. When Union flags start appearing on the streets of Northern Ireland, one can be sure that the Protestants there are feeling insecure.

The British tend to believe that ideas work best when they have been dissolved into the bloodstream of society to the point where they become second nature. Ideally, it would no more be possible to question the institution of monarchy than it would be to question the fact that one had kneecaps. Like breathing, ideas are what give life to a civilisation, but like the lungs they are in full working order only when we are unconscious of them. It is preferable not to drag such ideas into the light of day, where they can be wrangled over and contested. Perhaps they will no longer work if we become too aware of them, as juggling does not work if you think about it too much.

America, by contrast, tends to wear its ideology on its sleeve, which for the British is where it is least effective. Even some of its place names are ideologically charged: Hope, Zion, Providence and the like. Even "New England" is an article of faith as well as a name, meaning among other things better than the old England. Perhaps there is a town in Nevada called Market Forces, or one in Michigan called Nukecuba. The United States has not had as long as Britain to bed down its ruling ideas in everyday experience. This is one reason why it has to keep proclaiming them so loudly. It is also because some of the ideals in question are so sublime that they are hard to attain without constant exhortation.

De Tocqueville believed that general ideas were more prevalent in America than they were in Britain, which is one reason why Americans can speak of concepts like God and freedom less shamefacedly than the British. When the English generalise, he observed tartly, it is in spite of themselves. Those who have tried to circulate cultural and political theories in England can testify to the justness of this judgement. Aristocracies, de Tocqueville considered, tend to think not in terms of general humanity but in terms of specific families, places and traditions. Democratic societies like America are more likely to think in universal terms. Certainly the modern United States has an unfortunate habit of confusing its own national interests with those of humankind in general, not to speak of those of the Creator.

SIX

The One and the Many

Uniting the Nation

The United States of America is a peculiarly self-involved soci-ety, and outside the State Department is too little aware of other nations. It is a cosmopolitan power which can sometimes display the parochial outlook of a medieval peasant. In fact, much of its acquaintance with other countries has been down the barrel of a gun. Americans say quaint things like "Bangkok, Thailand," which nobody else in the world does, no doubt because their more untutored compatriots might imagine that Bangkok is in the Democratic Republic of Congo. Perhaps the United States invades other countries as a way of giving its citizens a much-needed geography lesson. Deciding to flatten Baghdad is a great incentive to finding out where it is.

The States also has a country too much like it directly to the north, and one too little like it directly to the south. It is true that Canadians see themselves as different from Americans, and so they are, but they are not always as different as they like to imagine.

"Americans have no neighbours," observed Alexis de Tocqueville. This is not literally true, of course, as one who was once arrested on the Mexican-American border can testify. Even so, it is interesting to speculate on how different the United States might be if it was cheek by jowl with a nation whose culture differed sharply from its own, yet with which it felt it had equal status. France and Germany are a case in point. Perhaps then it might be less self-preoccupied and more self-critical. To see yourself from the outside, it is inadvisable to have an enormous ocean stretching on either side of you.

The only other nations which never stop brooding on themselves are small ones. They are countries too much under the heel of a more powerful state, or too recently escaped from its shadow, to be completely assured of their identities. Whereas the English talk unceasingly of the weather, the Welsh speak incessantly of Wales. This is because the English conquered the Welsh and not vice versa. Any pub table of Irish intellectuals is mathematically certain to be wrangling over Irishness. Scottishness is as much a commodity as shortbread in Edinburgh or Aberdeen. National identity becomes an issue when something has gone awry with it, just as one's body becomes a talking point when it breaks down.

America's self-consciousness also springs from the fact that, being such an ethnic hodge-podge, it needs to proclaim a singular identity more insistently than, say, China or Denmark. Hence the panoply of flags, emblems, slogans and insignia. No household in Ireland would fly the national flag except perhaps as a joke, or because their rugby team was about to be hammered yet again by France. Houses in Britain which fly flags tend to display not the Union Jack but the St. George's flag, a gesture which can have racist implications. America, however, seems a country which is always about to fly centrifugally apart, fragmenting into its various social classes and ethnic subcultures, and is thus always in need of being pulled centripetally together. There is no such necessity in a minuscule place like Ireland, where the problem is not one of fragmentation but of too much homogeneity. Everyone in the country was at school with everyone else, and the grandfather of the optician across the street probably shot dead your own grandmother's butcher during the civil war that followed upon national independence. Irish memory goes a long way back: a friend of mine in Dublin had an acquaintance who served Mass for a man who saw the invading French fleet land in Ireland in 1798.

Small nations tend to breed cronyism, corruption, mutual contempt, envy, backbiting, back-scratching, and (supposedly the besetting Irish vice) begrudgery. Their conflicts are often the upshot of being too intimate with each other, not too estranged. "Great hatred, little room," as W. B. Yeats wrote of Ireland. America's problem, by contrast, is to hammer some unity out of those sublime spaces and astronomical distances, a project which can be achieved after a fashion by conspiracy theories. In a nation as unimaginably large and complex as the United States, it is gratifying to feel that the whole thing is somehow intended—that it is shaped by a secret but coherent design, such as the fact that Western governments have entered into a clandestine agreement with the Arab world to undermine conservative Christian values by flooding the West with Muslim immigrants. Quite why Western governments should indulge in such pointlessly self-destructive behaviour is not immediately apparent, but the theory at least has the virtue of turning a formless mass of events into a shapely narrative. It is far more enthralling than the boring view that Muslim immigrants are just coming to the States to find work.

In conspiracy theories, as in detective stories and the paranoid mind, a sneeze is never just a sneeze but a symptom of some deeper, invisible march of events. Conspiracy theories see the world as too stuffed with meaning, and in doing so compensate for a reality which is too bereft of it. Better to glimpse a sinister purpose everywhere you look than to face the fact that nothing means anything. Human beings are ready to will anything at all, Nietzsche remarked, rather than to make do with meaninglessness. People who seem to live permanently on the grassy knoll in Dallas in order to hand out leaflets full of gobbledygook are a case in point. There are, of course, plenty of conspiracies. Lots of people gather secretly in smoke-free rooms to plot the downfall of their opponents. One should not be so sophisticated about conspiracies as to be ridiculously naive. It is just that there is no one big overall conspiracy, any more than there is one big shoe factory which supplies everybody with their footwear. There is no one big conspiracy not only because it would be hard to run, but because there is no need for it.

One way of unifying a nation is to bring it together around certain common values. The phrase "American values" is commonly heard in the United States. It includes freedom and democracy, but also tolerance, equality and a faith in progress. The only problem is that there is no such thing as American values, any more than there is such a thing as Tibetan or Tahitian values. No nation has a monopoly on decency, justice, humanity and compassion. It is true that some countries stress certain values more than others. Arabs, for example, place a high value on hospitality, while the British place a high value on cocker spaniels. For the Swiss, concealing the bank accounts of the super-rich from the eyes of tax inspectors is a particularly time-honoured custom. But freedom is not inherently American, or hospitality peculiarly Arab. What an Iranian schoolteacher wants for her children is pretty much what a Californian bank clerk wants. One should recognise cultural differences, but not make a fetish of them.

There is a sense in which the United States has been far too successful in uniting its people. The tone, rhythm, and cadence in which the waitress says "You're all set" or "Have a good one" in Lincoln, Nebraska, are eerily identical to those you will hear in St. Cloud, Minnesota, and this in a nation for which diversity is supposed to be a supreme good. Another example of sameness is American handwriting, which is more uniform than the European variety. One can sometimes know one has received a letter from the USA before one has looked at the stamp. Styles of handwriting in Europe tend to start out roughly the same but then wildly diverge, whereas there is a way of forming one's letters as a child which tends to stick with Americans as they grow up. Now that keyboards have supplanted script, the uniformity is complete. De Tocqueville thought that the homogeneity of America springs from the fact that the same motive—love of money—lies at the root of everything its citizens do, and soon makes them "wearisome to contemplate." Industry, he points out, demands regular habits and tends to breed monotony. It is, he adds perceptively, the very vehemence of America's desire for possessions that makes it such a methodical place. It is a zeal which "agitates their minds but disciplines their lives." This is yet another way in which the country combines restlessness and regulation.

Forms and Traditions

In Europe, traditions, conventions and social forms have traditionally played a part in forging nations into one. This is less true of the United States, a country which is restive with form and convention and has a rather cavalier attitude to tradition. Instead, innovation is what Americans are supremely good at. They rank among the most inventive, imaginative people ever to have walked the earth. The British instinct is to fit into an established mould, conform to a given model, whereas the American impulse is to break the mould and create a fresh model. Americans are natural avant-gardists.

Take, for example, the business of American names. If you want to call yourself Dongo or Duckegg, what does it matter that nobody else ever has? Why should names be confined to a few traditional, mouth-filling sounds (William, George, Mary, Charles, Elizabeth), as with the British royal family? Why not have a king called Dave or a queen called Tracey? Why not call your pet tortoise Immanuel Kant? It is a sign of a society free from the fetters of tradition that Americans can call their children anything they like. Bash, Blip, Burp, Chugger, Palsy, Bladder, Pepper, Cruddingsworth, Dimple, Aorta: all these are possibilities. If you want to give your child a sixteen-syllable name, what is there to stop you? After all, British names can be a good deal more long-winded than American ones. The marriage was recently announced in London between Sir James Lockett Charles Agnew-Somerville and Lady Lucy Katherine Fortescue Gore, daughter of the Earl and Countess of Arran. The higher you are in the British social hierarchy, the more names you tend to accumulate, as well as the more vintage cars and landed estates.

The British have the uneasy feeling that some American names are the wrong way round. They suspect that someone called Houston B. Thomas should actually be called Thomas B. Houston, but that some unfortunate error occurred at the baptismal ceremony. This is because there are not many British first names that sound like second names. One suspects that some American names are straightforward mistakes. A woman called Meave recently appeared on U.S. television. Reverse the second and third letters and you have a familiar Irish name, but otherwise it is a complete innovation. There is surely a woman somewhere in the United States called Verjinnia, just as there are probably one or two small boys called Enry running around Manchester. A couple I knew in the States were intending to give their son the Irish name Padraic. Since they pronounced it phonetically (it is actually pronounced "Porrick"), it is perhaps fortunate that they changed their minds.

For the British, tradition is a kind of labour-saving device. Like an efficient private secretary, it does a good deal of unobtrusive work on your behalf. It makes certain routine decisions about your life, thus leaving you free to devote your time and energy to something more rewarding. Tradition has decreed that the House of Windsor could not possibly call a son Vince or a daughter Gladys. This means that the royal family does not have to sit around cudgelling their brains over the question, but can get on with more important matters, such as killing harmless animals in the Scottish Highlands. You do not have to spend time fretting about whether to wear evening dress or a rabbit costume at a state banquet, since tradition has decided this for you in advance.

The great majority of men and women who have ever inhabited the planet have lived in tradition, and many of them still do. Non-traditional living is a recent invention. The collective wisdom of your ancestors was plainly a more reliable guide to how to live than any bright idea you might happen to stumble across yourself in a stray moment of inspiration. In this sense, there is a certain humility about a faith in tradition. Most of what you need to know is already available. God would not have been so outrageously inconsiderate as to fail to let us know from the outset all the truths necessary for our salvation. It is inconceivable that he might forget to tell us not to fornicate, and then belatedly plant this idea in the mind of some moralist around 1905. Innovation for the traditionalist mind is to be treated warily, and usually turns out to be bogus. Every so-called novelty is simply a minor variation on things that have existed from the origin of time. There is no idea that had not been anticipated by others. Most of our knowledge is a footnote to the ancients. There are probably proposals for Reality TV and hints on motorcycle maintenance in some lost manuscript of Aristotle. Any lecturer who declares that toothpaste was invented in the modern age is simply asking for trouble. A tube of the stuff is bound to turn up three weeks later in a Mayan temple.

Tradition, then, relieves you of some of your freedom of

choice, which some Americans find objectionable. They prefer
to see their lives as a series of strenuously self-defining decisions.
This has some positive political implications. What is important
in a liberal democracy is less what you decide than the fact that
you decide. This is an admirable kind of politics, if also a somewhat adolescent one. Teenagers sometimes feel that being able
to make their own decisions matters more than the decisions
they make. The oddness of political democracy has not been
sufficiently appreciated. It means embracing the possibility of
false, even disastrous decisions simply because they are ours. We
would reject the idea of an enlightened despotism even if we
knew in advance that the policies it came up with would be far
wiser than those we might concoct ourselves. This is extraordinary, but also perfectly proper. Human beings may misuse their
freedom, but they are not truly human without it.

Americans suspect that to hand over your choices to tradition or convention is to be inauthentic. Forms are Catholic,
while personal decisions are Protestant. Rites and conventions
are what link people together for Europeans, and what intrude
between them for Americans. A grotesque caricature of an
American General in Dickens's novel *Martin Chuzzlewit* cries
sorrowfully, "But, oh the conventionalities of that a-mazing
Europe! . . . The exclusiveness, the pride, the form, the ceremony. . . . The artificial barriers set up between man and man;
the division of the human race into court cards and plain cards,
of every denomination, into clubs, diamonds, spades, anything
but hearts!" Form in America is at war with feeling. This is why
a folksy remark in a formal setting can get you elected president.
Conventions are stiff, heartless, recalcitrant affairs. They must
be continually broken and remade to bring them into line with

one's changing experience. Why not call your child Blip before lunch and Cruddingsworth after dinner?

Traditions and conventions are impersonal, which for Europeans is what allows them to bring different kinds of people together. For Americans, however, they smack too little of the warm-blooded individual spirit. Individualist societies tend to find social forms unreal, even though there would be no individuals without them. Manners in America, writes de Tocqueville, "form, as it were, a thin, transparent veil through which the real feelings and personal thoughts of each man can be easily seen." They are "hampering veils put between [Americans] and the truth." Forms are valid only if they are directly expressive of content. Otherwise, there is something brittle and arthritic about them. America delights in the rough-diamond cop or sheriff who is driven by his humanity to throw away the rulebook and violate all the procedures. Heroes and outlaws in the States can be hard to tell apart. There is sometimes little to choose between the visionary and the vigilante.

This has its undoubted virtues. There is a European fetishism of forms about which America feels rightly uneasy. My Cambridge tutor used to refuse to shake hands with his pupils during the vacations, as this apparently contravened some arcane, medieval regulation. If we wished to consult him in his capacity as an officer of the university, rather than as a college tutor, we were obliged to leave his room and come in again. Americans would rightly consider such behaviour a form of insanity. They refuse to sacrifice feeling to form, an attitude from which Europe has much to learn.

Yet a casualness about forms can overlook the fact that rules and procedures exist to protect the vulnerable as well as shield the privileged. In Robert Bolt's play about Sir Thomas More, *A Man for All Seasons*, More's impetuous son-in-law Roper declares that he would "cut down every law in Europe to get at the Devil himself." "Oh?" replies More. "And when the last law was down, and the Devil turned round on you, where would you hide, the laws all being flat? This country's planted thick with laws from coast to coast—Man's laws, not God's—and if you cut them down—and you're just the man to do it—d'you really think you could stand upright in the winds that would blow then?" Roper's attitude is Protestant, while More's case is Catholic. More is a touch too respectful of laws and forms, while Roper sees them simply as impediments. There are a lot of hot-headed young Ropers in American movies.

As far as formality goes, the Dickens of *American Notes* is startled by an American who "constantly walked in and out of the room with his hat on; and stopped to converse in the same free-and-easy state; and lay down on our sofa, and pulled out his newspaper from his pocket, and read it at his ease." Wearing a hat scarcely strikes us nowadays as free and easy, though Dickens obviously finds the act of wearing one indoors, not to speak of addressing someone else while doing so, a faintly startling example of American laid-backness. He should, he adds, be offended by such customs back home, but charitably overlooks them in the as yet embryonic nation across the Atlantic.

Formality can indeed be constrictive, but America's distaste for it means that dignity is not what it does best. Three young women who appeared on U.S. television recently to plead for the arrest of their brother's killer seemed like any other young people in the world assigned such a mournful task, except that all three of them were chewing gum. Allusions to slam dunks and home runs are ritually inserted into serious political commentary. Sporting metaphors infiltrate official language far more than they do in Europe. When George W. Bush spoke on television, it did not seem out of the question that he might suddenly pull a toy fire engine out of his pocket and run it up and down his sleeve while making *brrmm-brrmm* noises. A lack of gravitas is the price Americans pay for their attractive ease of manner. If Barack Obama is an untypical American, it is not because he is a closet socialist or was born on Venus, but because he is able to be relaxed and dignified at the same time.

Soft Cosmos

Forms and traditions, then, cannot be relied upon to unite the nation. They constrain personal choice, and constraint in the United States, except when it comes to locking up child pickpockets for three consecutive life terms, is in general frowned on. It is part of the affirmative spirit of the nation that there are few given restrictions in human life. Some restraints, regrettably, are essential, but for the most part they are limits we impose on ourselves, and thus testify ironically to our freedom. If I handcuff my wrists, lock myself in a sack and hang myself upside down from the ceiling for a year or so, my liberty is not fundamentally affected. After all, I did it all myself.

To the medieval mind, the only truly unconstrained being was God. Yet if God's freedom was to be perfect, it could not be confined by the world he had created. If it was, he would not be all-powerful. He would be as much constrained as we are by the fact that blood coagulates, or that you can hire a horse and carriage in Luxor. Some medieval thinkers therefore taught that God was no respecter of the logic of his own Creation. Because he made the world, he could do what he liked with it. It was his private property, and he could annihilate it tomorrow, or turn it into an enormous Barbie doll, just as you are free to rip your priceless Rubens to pieces if the fancy takes you. It was this way of seeing, one which made much of the supremacy of God's will, that was to win out in the modern period. After a while, the divine will was replaced by the human one. The world was now our private property, to be disposed of as we wished.

On this view, there is no necessity to the way things are. If there were, then God would be subject to the laws of his own universe. In fact, however, he suffers no such indignity. If he grows bored with fire being hot, the royal family being cold, or Clint Eastwood being right-wing, he can always take these things back to the laboratory and redesign them. There is nothing necessary about fire being hot. In another of God's universes it might be freezing. It is like that only because God arbitrarily decided that it should be. He could turn Glenn Beck into a bleeding-heart liberal if the fancy took him. Fox TV does not run training camps for Palestinian guerrillas only because God has whimsically decreed that it should not.

American ideology aspires to this Godlike freedom. There is a sense in which it is less concerned to worship the Creator than to take his place. It is now we, not he, who determine how things are. There is, however, a price to be paid for this privilege. What is valuable is what the will invests with value. But since this is pretty arbitrary, it comes close to admitting that there is no real value at all. Besides, how can we know that the will itself is valuable? We would seem incapable of coming up with some external standard by which to judge it. Another price human beings have to pay for this supreme sovereignty is that things no longer have integral identities of their own. To think so is the thought crime of "essentialism." Their identities are in constant flux, always on the point of transmuting into something else as the whimsical will may decide. The flipside of a faith in the world's plasticity is a belief in the dominative mind. If the will is to be omnipotent, reality must be softened up. It is the will, not forms and traditions, which dictates how the world should be. Yet there are many millions of such wills, all with different purposes. So how is the nation to be unified?

On this view, things are what we make them, a article of faith to which some of the early American settlers clung. The belief crops up again in modern-day relativism. I have taught highly intelligent American graduate students who believe that there are as many truths as there are individuals. If you are committed to the view that tapioca is a grain used in puddings, and I think it is a rather beautiful island in the Caribbean, both of us are right from our different points of view. This is simply one example of how postmodernism can addle the brains. Even truth has been privatised. Nor is this a recent American prejudice. As de Tocqueville comments, "each man is narrowly shut up in himself, and from that basis makes the pretension to judge the world." What you make of the world is not what I make of it. So freedom is at odds with consensus. It is hard to pluck an *unum* out of this *pluribus*, as the motto of the United States imagines we can.

The positive aspect of all this is its Protestant respect for individual judgement. My judgement may not be as sound as yours in practice, but it is certainly as good in principle. Beneath this view lies a deeply admirable egalitarianism. Yet if all of us are right in a way that admits of no argument, the only way we can decide the issue may be by fighting over it. Relativism can lead to violence. It is true that Oscar Wilde once described art as a phenomenon in which one thing can be true but also its opposite, but you can get away in art with things you cannot get away with in life, as Wilde was to learn to his cost.

De Tocqueville sees a link between America's belief in infinite striving and its ethic of equality. In hierarchical societies, your rank defines your limits. It sketches the contours of the possible. The behaviour of an ancient Athenian rope maker was constrained by the requirement that he behave like an ancient Athenian rope maker. Where rank is less of an issue, anything seems conceivable, and the scope of human perfectibility, in de Tocqueville's words, "is stretched beyond reason." The typical citizen of such societies is "searching always, falling, picking himself up again, often disappointed, never discouraged."

As far as rank goes, one might add that though the United States today is a grotesquely unequal society, its everyday culture is a good deal more egalitarian than that of Britain. There is a genuine classlessness about America's behaviour, if not about its property structure. Like American frankness, pleasantness and sociability, this oils the wheels of social intercourse. By contrast, it is almost impossible for two Britons to meet without each of them instantly picking up the class signals emitted by the other, like animals who send each other messages in the form of low drones or high-pitched squeakings. To be sure after two minutes' conversation that your companion attended an expensive private school is almost within the capacity of a British six-year-old. To know which school he attended requires a finer attunement of one's social antennae, but is not out of the question.

Throwing out hierarchies, however, is more than just a political matter in the States. It is also a way of seeing the world. Things do not spontaneously sort themselves into an order of priorities. For some extreme versions of this viewpoint, nothing is inherently more significant than anything else, rather as a duke is not innately superior to a bootblack. In one sense, this is a deeply liberating attitude. It frees America from the gradations and exclusions of old Europe. It can break out of these rigid rankings to revaluate the whole of reality. This takes a degree of boldness and vision, and the United States has both in plenty. At the same time, there are limits to this outlook. Hierarchies of value die hard. It is difficult not to feel that curing leprosy is more important than powdering one's nose. Much as one may hate being a hierarchicalist, one has to acknowledge a sneaking preference for preventing genocide over promoting the sale of jelly beans. Perhaps it is better to confess that one is sadly unreconstructed and try as hard as one can to find Rod Stewart as talented as Regina Spektor.

The anti-elitist spirit is part of America's rejection of the Old World, in which everyone had an allotted place and was expected to keep to it. Against this, the United States believes in a radical equality of being. It is true that the American Dream, with its faith that anyone can scramble to the top, sounds rather more generous than it actually is. Anyone can jump off the Golden Gate Bridge as well, but not many actually do. (It is a sociological fact, incidentally, that those who do so tend to jump off facing the city of San Francisco rather than facing away from it.) "Anyone" sounds excitingly close to "everyone," but it is also depressingly close to "no-one." All the same, individuals could now be judged for themselves, not respected simply because they were the nephew of a count.

Once again, however, there are drawbacks to this doctrine. A doorman is as good as an arch-duke, and a piece of paper blown about by the breeze is as good as the end of the slave trade if that is what you believe. Everyone makes their own choices and sets their own priorities. What I say goes, and what you say goes as well, even if the two are mutually contradictory. It is better to be self-contradictory than exclusive. To be selective is to be elitist. This is why the great postmodern mantra is inclusivity. Nobody should ever be left out. Slave traffickers, the White Kentucky Riflemen for Jesus, and people who snatch your glasses jeeringly from your nose and scamper off with them down the street: all have their place in the great disorder of things. To shut out is to be negative, and negativity is among the most heinous of moral crimes. One can be criticised in the States for being critical.

Picking and Mixing

If everything is as good as everything else, then all these things can be exchanged with one another. In economic life, this is known as the market. Nothing is more hostile to hierarchy than the commodity. No way of life is more diverse, pluralistic and transgressive than capitalism. It is as promiscuous as a porn star and as non-discriminatory as the most tender-hearted liberal. In its all-generous spirit, it wishes to exclude nobody and nothing. It treats all doormen like arch-dukes if they are potential consumers. A can opener is as good as a defibrillator if it can reap you as much profit. It is never easy in the United States to draw the line between generosity of spirit and sheer sloppiness, the open-minded and the scatterbrained.

America was originally considered a wilderness. It was a random, chaotic chunk of reality in which there were no established relations between things. You could thus make of these things more or less what you wanted, as God himself could for some medieval thought. They had come loose from any set pattern, and could be permutated as you saw fit. This, no doubt, is one source of the eclecticism of modern American culture, which pitches different bits of reality indifferently together. In this sense, there is a connection between the Puritan world view and surf 'n' turf. Eclecticism goes a good way back in American history. In *American Notes*, Charles Dickens describes a meal he had with a number of Americans that consisted of "tea, coffee, bread, butter, salmon, shad, liver, steak, potatoes, pickles, ham, chops, black puddings, and sausages. . . . Some [of the Americans] were fond of compounding this variety, and having it all on their plates at once."

An even more bizarre compound was recently consumed by an American citizen. It consisted of two chicken-fried steaks with gravy and sliced onions; a triple-patty bacon cheeseburger; a cheese omelette with ground beef, tomato, onions, bell peppers and jalapenos; a bowl of fried okra with ketchup; one pound of barbecued meat with half a loaf of white bread; three fajitas; a meat-lover's pizza; one pint of Blue Bell ice cream; a slab of peanut-butter fudge with crushed peanuts; and three root beers. This was the last meal of a death row prisoner in Texas awaiting his lethal injection, a demand so outrageous that it led to calls for the custom of tailor-made last meals to be abolished. One likes to imagine that the prisoner in question was a satirist. Perhaps he intended to beat the needle with a carefully timed coronary.

Like a popular singles bar, the United States is a place which teems with infinite possibility. It does not just contain pockets of fantasies like Hollywood and Disneyland, but is in some ways a full-blown fantasy in itself. In America, de Tocqueville remarks, "something which does not exist is just something that has not been tried yet." Fictions are just facts waiting to happen. The nation does not accept that a shadow may fall between the conception and the execution. Because the mind is what matters, anything you dream up is as good as done. All you need is will-power. This is one of several ways in which America is a godly nation. God, too, is thought to manifest no gap between the possible and the actual. His thoughts are his deeds. He does not sit around biting his fingernails and wondering whether to bring Jack Nicholson down with a nasty bout of flu.

The line between fact and fantasy continually wavers. Fiction can be truer than reality, as the career of Charlie Sheen exemplifies. Sheen, who despite his dishevelled private life is an immensely talented actor, is much more real in front of the cameras than he is in reality. Reality for him is largely fantasy. It is only when he is acting that he can be himself. Only the act of transporting himself into fiction can impose enough discipline and coherence on his personality for him to come truly alive. Otherwise he dissolves into a soggy mess of conflicting moods and impulses. His shambolic off-stage persona is a mere shadow of his genuine, fictional self. Those who have too few restraints tend to fall apart, which is not what the doctrinaire free marketeers want to hear. Some bits of American reality strike an observer as blatantly fictitious. One hears that there is to be a federal investigation into whether Donald Trump is a real or imaginary character. The Dickensian resonance of his surname points to a likely conclusion. One or two celebrities who have been frozen out of Britain for illicitly masquerading as real people have made their mark in the United States.

It is a commonplace that Americans tend to describe what happens in the real world by reference to movies. Life exists to imitate art. An American to whom I once showed the half-timbered Tudor buildings of Stratford-upon-Avon high street exclaimed: "Great shot!" Artistic dreamers try to tell it like it is, while hard-nosed Wall Street stockbrokers manifest a kind of communal madness. Life in the transnational corporations becomes more surreal than a Buñuel film. The world of business was once associated with sober realism, but nowadays it is closer in some respects to a crazed religious cult. From time to time, it acts out the economic equivalent of collective suicide. Corporate executives are admonished to ignore unpalatable facts and disavow inconvenient problems. Mao would have been proud of their delusional zeal. Realism is socialistic and unpatriotic. There are times when self-deception and megalomaniacal self-belief oust rational decision-making altogether. To complete the inversion, religious cults hire teams of chief executives, remove crosses from their churches in case they send too negative a message, and rebrand worshippers as customers.

Scientists who hold that there is an infinity of different universes envisage a situation in which anything that can happen, will happen. Somewhere in the so-called multiverse of the astrophysicists, someone looking unnervingly like you, maybe even endowed with your name, is at this moment reading these words, written by someone looking uncannily like me. Perhaps there are an infinite number of such acts occurring right now. This, to be sure, has some depressing implications. It means, for example, that there is an infinity of Mel Gibsons and Paris Hiltons. There is also an unlimited number of Michael Jacksons, not all of them dead. But it is not all bad news. Somewhere in the cosmos, someone looking suspiciously like Bill O'Reilly is at this very moment wearing a Fidel Castro outfit and arguing the necessity of soaking the rich. On earth, this infinity of worlds is known as the United States. Among other marvels, it contains a world which looks just like ours but where everything is bigger. This is known as Texas.

Whereas Jesus multiplied loaves and fishes, the United States multiplies options. No restaurant in Britain would ask you how you liked your fried eggs, any more than they would ask you what exotic national costume you would like your waiter to be dressed in. Choice in the States is a paramount value. "I've made my choices" is a common American phrase, meaning among other things that one is the author of one's own existence rather than ignominiously shaped by circumstance. Life is a self-authoring narrative in which, unlike Oedipus or Anna Karenina, you get to decide what happens to you. It is therefore all the more surprising that there is so little political choice in the country. In fact, the United States is a one-party state. There is the Democratic capitalist party and the Republican capitalist party. The diversity of political options hardly rivals the variety of candy bars.

Somewhere at this moment, some American, perhaps several of them in different places, is trying to sell life insurance to a Vietnamese orphan while wearing a false red nose, clown's flippers and a loud check suit. In the United States, anything that can be imagined, however outlandish, has an excellent chance of existing. "I can think of it, therefore it exists" is the American version of Descartes's dictum. If you can think of making a new kind of ice cream out of tea leaves soaked in squirrel's urine, you can be sure that someone in the States is trying to patent it at this very moment. One can imagine a musical in which the staff of a restaurant burst into song every time one of them is tipped, but in the States this actually happens. The country represents a constant translation of the subjunctive (what might happen) into the indicative (what is the case).

If there is no order in the world, and if all its parts are equal and interchangeable, then you can will into existence any combination of these parts you like, and the act of willing makes it acceptable. The United States is the kind of place where one expects to find hairdressers selling sea food, or pastors doubling up as plumbers. In one sense, this is a distinct improvement on Britain, where you might find yourself having to buy a flashlight in one store and a battery for it in another. Americans tend to sling together items that Europeans would keep strictly apart. They do not understand that it has been ordained by a wise, all-loving Creator that while marmalade is acceptable at breakfast, jam (or jelly) is not. If you want to wear canary yellow trousers with an electric blue blouse, there is nothing to stop you. If you want to believe in Marx and the tooth fairy simultaneously, then go ahead. There are no natural fitnesses in things, no given constraints that must not be transgressed. Things that should not be put together, like the Oval Office and persons of low intelligence, sometimes are. Occasionally, things that should be put together are not. Some Americans are ignorant of the natural law that forbids the wearing of jeans without belts. The widespread American use of the word "whatever" indicates that precision and distinction are not held in the highest regard. It betrays how close the indiscriminate is to the indifferent. De Tocqueville thought such eclecticism was also true of American English, which mixed the vulgar and the refined without discrimination. It came, he thought, from the pitching together of social strata which in Europe would stay strictly separate.

If one thing is valuable, and so is another, then it is arithmetically self-evident that to have them both is even more of a good thing. Sikh turbans are cool, and so are Scottish kilts, so why not wear them both together? Why not have it all rather than settle for half? The European instinct is for either/or, while the American impulse is for both/and. Americans are open to new configurations of experience, while Europeans suspect that the new will simply turn out to be a recycled version of the old. America is a genuinely path-breaking nation which has always had the boldness to embrace the unfamiliar. This, however, has come to mean that newness in the States is a value in itself—a curious belief, since fascism was an innovation in its time, and the Spanish Inquisition was remarkably up-to-date. The course of human history is strewn with repellent novelties.

If something is good, then it also follows that it is good to have as much of it as possible. Limits are taboo in this sense as well. Why settle for a steak as big as your fist when you could have one the size of Chris Christie? The American appetite is in this sense no more restrained than American speech is reticent. The nation sees little beauty in sparseness or symmetry. Amplitude is valued over leanness. Extravagance wins out over elegance. Nor does the country seem to appreciate the fact that appetites can be pleasurably enhanced by being curbed, as the naked body is more seductive when it is suggestively veiled. If there is so much obesity in the United States, it is among other things because the idea that you should eat only as much as is good for you suggests a standard independent of one's appetites, which is a distinctly suspect notion. There can be no objective yardstick in the marketplace. You cannot get outside your own desires and judge them from an external standpoint, since desire is what you are made of. Desire is its own measure.

The Fine and the Good

Old and New Worlds

Europeans are fine, while Americans are good. This, at least, would seem to be the opinion of Henry James, who knew both civilisations from the inside and never ceased to compare them. Europe for James is the home of style, form, evil, civility, enjoyment, corruption, surface, experience, artifice and exploitation. America is the land of innocence, substance, earnestness, integrity, barrenness, nature, monotony and morality. The European self is diverse, fuzzy at the edges, saturated in history and culture; the American self is raw, solid and unified, and lives in an eternal present. As puritans, Americans are hyperconscious of evil, but they are largely free of it themselves. The strenuous moral conscience that alerts them to it also shields them against it. As an American character remarks in *The Europeans*, those around her have nothing to repent of and yet are always repenting. James himself comments of Emerson's writing that it has "no sense of the dark, the foul, the base," which one might have thought was more of a compliment than a criticism. Yet it is not intended to be.

Even so, James associates Americans with evil in the sense that their innocence and good nature tend to attract it. The fresh-faced American heiress on the loose in Europe can easily fall prey to civilised predators. The problem with Americans, as James sees it, is that they are innocent yet avid for experience, which makes them especially vulnerable to being abused by wicked adventurers. It is hard to have an innocence which also looks out for itself. If Americans were guileless but stayed at home, or if they ventured abroad but had a sharp eye for deceivers, all would be well. It is the combination of innocence and a hunger for experience which is so dangerous, not least if you happen to be fabulously well-off. So, as long as there are rapacious types around, there will also be a need for tedious, high-toned moralists.

In this as in other ways, moralist and immoralist are sides of the same coin. The good tend not to be stylish and amusing, and this can count heavily against them. They are commendable but not charming. But this may be the price they have to pay for not injuring others. It is a fearsomely steep price, not least in the eyes of the supremely stylish James, but you cannot quarrel with it in the end. In the end, the good must win out over the fine. Yet it is the fine who make life worth living. If you have to choose between style and substance, then you must go for substance. But the fact that you have to choose in the first place suggests that something is amiss.

Europe is a civilisation rich in experience, but one that is somehow tainted. Guilt and corruption are never far from the coruscating surfaces of social life. Because they are more "aesthetic" than Americans, more taken with form, pleasure, and a dazzling play of appearances, Europeans look at the world with the detached, wryly amused stance of an artistic observer, and this can prove morally irresponsible. They can also treat other people as aesthetic objects. Art is the fullest way to live, but it is never far from exploitation. It is also never far from a sort of sterility, one which is ironically close to the way James sees so much everyday American existence. Art must radiate a sense of how to live; but it may be that the artist can achieve this only by devoting himself religiously to his art, and thus, ironically, failing to live himself.

Art for James is a constant self-sacrifice. It involves giving the self away, not noisily asserting it in the manner of entrepreneurial America. If being an artist means not living to the full, then art is a kind of failure and vacancy, as well as a supreme expression of human life. It is not on the side of the success ethic. There is thus a sense in which art is un-American. It is also un-American because it involves the tragedy of the unfulfilled self. Yet this may not be the whole story. One of James's most acute insights is his sense of how close self-abandonment may be to a kind of selfishness. It is hard to say whether some of his characters are behaving with beautiful disinterestedness or brutal egoism. They may be either martyrs or monsters. So art, which involves self-sacrifice, may not be all that far from self-interest after all.

If Europe and America were simple opposites, things would be relatively straightforward. But for James this is by no means true. Culture of the European kind is the product of leisure, and leisure is the product of labour. Only by the kind of Protestant work ethic for which America is renowned can you pile up enough wealth to set people free for the higher things in life. Only if the many toil away in their workshops can the few stroll the art galleries of Florence and Vienna. In this sense, civilised values rest on violence and exploitation. The European virtues are dependent on the American ones. The two places are not such opposites after all. Civility means the kind of gracious living that has lost sight of its own murky origins. If it could recall them—if it lacked this saving blind spot—it might not be able to survive.

The point is to have so much money that you don't need to think about it. Having an enormous amount of wealth sets you free from wealth. It grants you the time instead to note how the fragrance of lilies drifts through the gathering dusk, or how the light from a stained glass window dapples the ample bodice of a duchess. So, the more the American values of industry and self-discipline thrive, the more the European virtues will flourish. Yet the opposite is true as well. The more ruthlessly acquisitive people become, the more civilised values come under siege. The process of amassing wealth threatens to undermine the fine living that can result from it. Life is more agreeable if you are rich, but actually making money is not particularly agreeable.

James moved in the kind of social world in which you can see that a man and a woman must be having an affair because when you come across them alone in a drawing room, he is sitting down while she is standing up. Yet in the chilling words of his secretary, Theodora Bosanquet, "When he walked out of the refuge of his study and into the world and looked about him, he saw a place of torment, where creatures of prey perpetually thrust their claws into the quivering flesh of doomed, defence-less children of light." In this cut-throat civilisation, the only way to avoid harming others may be to renounce life altogether. Or it may be to live vicariously, through the consciousness of others, as the artist does. Art is a way of engaging with life while keeping it at arm's length. It is the bitter fruit of never having really lived. It combines the American virtues of austerity and self-restraint with the European values of fine living.

Divided Nation

James, who died in 1916, was not to know that American and European values would become even more interwoven in the century after his death. One of the most striking paradoxes of the United States is that a nation of austere, industrious men and women gave birth to a culture of liberal values and rampant hedonism. In the end, all that draining of swamps and hacking down forests resulted in one of the world's great civilisations. It also resulted in Hugh Hefner and Ben & Jerry. Or, to put the point differently, industrial capitalism eventually yielded to consumer capitalism, as it did elsewhere in the world. Elsewhere, however, the contrast between the two is not always so glaring. Italy and Greece are consumer societies, but these nations were not founded by men in white collars and tall black hats who believed that enjoyment for its own sake was the work of the devil.

There is no mystery about how men in tall black hats ended up as cigar-chewing Hollywood moguls. Entertainment is big business. Adventure was converted into enterprise. You could consecrate the profane realm of pleasure by absorbing it into the sober domain of commerce. Rather as Henry James explored reality through the arm's-length device known as art, so you can engage with humour, drama, and sensual enjoyment through the arm's-length device known as profit. You must not wallow mindlessly in the senses, but it is alright to do so if it serves an abstract, rational end beyond itself, namely, the expansion of your capital.

The problem, however, is that consumer values in the States have not simply taken over from productive ones. For one thing, the consumer industry itself needs to be produced. For another thing, puritan values are far too robust to yield to strip joints without a struggle. They continue to flourish side by side with liberal and consumerist ones, which is what makes the United States such a chronically schizoid culture. How its citizens are required to act in the bedroom or boardroom is not at all how they are expected to behave in the disco or shopping mall. Regulation is taboo in the marketplace but mandatory in the home, school and public sphere. This is by no means true only of the United States, though it appears there in most graphic form. Modern capitalist societies make contradictory demands on their citizens, depending on whether they happen to be in the chapel or the casino. They call for conflicting kinds of subjectivity.

This is why the quarrel in Henry James between the plea-surable and the dutiful, or the liberal and authoritarian, is as relevant today as it was a century ago. It is just that it no longer takes the form of a clash between America and Europe. The conflict is much nearer to home than that. A new nation has been born in America, one far less hidebound than the old, but the old one survives alongside it. The centred, repressive, self-disciplined ego of production and puritan values is at war with the decentred, liberated, consumerist self. The two cultures can negotiate compromises from time to time, but there is no possibility of a perpetual peace between them. In some ways, their respective inhabitants are as alien to each other as the natives of Borneo are to the citizens of Berlin. No wonder the politicians keep loudly proclaiming that there is only one America. Whenever one hears declarations of unity, one knows that the situation must be dire indeed, rather as whenever one hears appeals for harmony one knows that someone's interests are under threat.

Modest Proposals

What should Americans do to be saved? They should start calling children children. They should try to think negatively. They should discover how to use a teapot. Learning how to mock themselves would be an incomparably greater achievement than landing on Mars. They should stop selling themselves as the finest country in the world because there is no such thing, any more than there are Gorgons and goblins. There should be compulsory courses for all college freshmen in how not to mean what you say. Americans should press their astonishing ignorance of abroad to the point where they can no longer invade other people's countries because all maps have been destroyed and all knowledge of geography made a criminal offence. They should stop underestimating elegance. They should learn that true power springs from a compact with frailty and failure. They should try to get on friendlier terms with their bodies.

Above all, they should stop making such a song and dance about salvation. They should try to be less moral, idealistic, earnest and high-minded. They should take a break from all that uplifting, inspiring, healing, empowering, dreaming, edifying and aspiring. Then they might be more admirable people. In many respects—in their friendliness, honesty, openness, inventiveness, courtesy, civic pride, ease of manner, generosity of spirit, and egalitarian manners—they are admirable enough already. But Americans are the first to admit that there is always room for improvement. It is an honourable puritan doctrine.

The good news about the citizens of this kindly, violent, bigoted, generous-spirited nation is that if ever the planet is plunged into nuclear war, they will be the first to crawl over the edge of the crater, dust themselves down, and proceed to build a new world. The bad news is that they will probably have started the war.

Acknowledgements

I am grateful to my friend Ray Ryan and my literary agent Georges Borchardt, both of whom helped with admirable efficiency to ease this book into the world. I must also thank John Glusman and Tori Leventhal at W. W. Norton for their splendidly scrupulous editing of the manuscript, and two of the Americans I hold in captivity, Willa Murphy and Oliver Eagleton, for saving me from some embarrassing blunders. I would like to be able to thank the other two captives as well, but at present they are both illiterate.

About the Author

TERRY EAGLETON was born in Salford, England, in 1943. He attended Trinity College, Cambridge, where he earned both an MA and a PhD. He is the author of more than forty books, including *Why Marx Was Right* and the seminal *Literary Theory: An Introduction*, as well as a novel, a film script, plays performed in London and Dublin, and a critically acclaimed memoir, *The Gatekeeper*. Eagleton has taught at Oxford, Cambridge, and the National University of Ireland, and most recently at the University of Notre Dame. He currently resides in Dublin with his wife and children.